Teaching

the

Ten Commandments

by

Sisters Mary Agnesine and Mary Catherine,
of the School Sisters of Notre Dame

ST. AUGUSTINE ACADEMY PRESS
HOMER GLEN, ILLINOIS

Nihil obstat,
  H. B. RIES,
    Censor librorum

Imprimatur,
  ✠ SAMUEL A. STRITCH,
    Archiepiscopus Milwauchiensis

January 9, 1931

This book was originally published in 1931
by The Bruce Publishing Company.

This facsimile edition reprinted in 2019
by St. Augustine Academy Press.

Stories in appendix taken from
The Sacred Heart Messenger, April 1929.

ISBN: 978-1-64051-100-2

INTRODUCTION

The separate publication of these lessons on the Ten Commandments of God by Sisters Agnesine and Catherine, S.S.N.D., from the *Catholic School Journal* is due to the extraordinary number of requests that have come for the numbers of the magazine which contained these articles. Our supply of the magazine is exhausted. Sister Mary Agnesine, S.S.N.D., prepared the material on the first, third, sixth, eighth, and ninth commandments. Sister Mary Catherine, S.S.N.D., prepared the material on the second, fourth, and fifth commandments. The two sisters collaborated on the study of the seventh and tenth commandments.

These articles, prepared by two specially competent teachers under the direction of the editor, aim to furnish a rich background for the study of the commandments. The essential doctrinal points are presented in outline form — this is the material ordinarily contained in the Catechism — but to show the possibili-'ies of the enrichment of the curriculum in religion, there is gathered a rich array of concrete cases from the home life and school life of the children, a suggestive list of pictures, poems, or quotations from the

Bible, an illustrative list of stories from the Old and New Testaments, examples of completion, false and true, and multiple answer tests, and appropriate memory gems for each commandment. What a rich array of additional content for material that seemed too often dead, but which has in it life — indeed, eternal life.

This rich array of material is suggestive as to method. Almost any example of this material might furnish a lead into the doctrine, or furnish an application of doctrine already learned. How enriched the doctrinal teaching will be if the practical cases are used in the approach, in the actual formulation of the truth of religion, and in their application. Sister Agnesine has emphasized in her part of the work the discussion method; Sister Catherine, though using informal methods of approach, is more didactic in spirit. With some teachers one approach will be better; for others, the other.

In any case the material has proved to be suggestive and practical, and we trust it will be found serviceable in this form to a wider group, who we trust too, may join our *Catholic School Journal Family*.

EDWARD A. FITZPATRICK

CONTENTS

THE FIRST COMMANDMENT[1]

The plan to be followed in this and succeeding lessons, is the one outlined in a study of the Eighth Commandment which appeared in the November (1929) number.[2] According to this plan, each pupil is expected to participate in solving the problems, in submitting new problems and experiences, and in making comments and suggestions for the benefit of the class. Two distinct advantages should be derived from such a method: In the first place, it should bring to light some of the erroneous opinions frequently held by pupils in regard to the simplest, oft-repeated truths of religion; and secondly, it offers opportunity to weigh and compare values, to interchange opinions and experiences, and so to become more deeply impressed with the lesson under discussion.

Experience has shown again and again that although pupils may know the truths of their religion very well, they often fail to apply them at the proper time. A group of seniors, most of whom had attended various Catholic schools all their lives, were discussing a play in which the hero, a criminal, lies about his identity, in order to shield his family from disgrace. One of the group raised the question as to whether he was justified

---

[1]For pupils of the upper grades.
[2]See the Eighth Commandment, p. 121.

in telling lies, and the great majority of pupils emphatically held that he was justified because he did it for so worthy a motive. It was only when they were asked whether they had ever heard it said that even if we could save the whole world by telling a single lie, we would not dare to do so, that they realized the mistake they had made. It must be remarked that the teacher herself did not ask the question as to whether the lies were justified or not, and also that the discussion did not take place during religion class. Results would probably have been different under the latter circumstances.

Approach to Discussion-Group Method

It may be in place to repeat here what has been said in another lesson; namely, that the teacher who wishes to make use of the discussion-group method, must approach the work with a great deal of sympathy and understanding and must be sure that she possesses the confidence of the children. An expression of surprise or of horror on the teacher's face when a pupil unconsciously and in good faith expresses an erroneous opinion, may forever kill the desire to contribute further to the class discussion. It must be understood, also, that the discussions be serious and purposeful, and *that definite conclusions be reached.* A simple, specific resolution, after the serious consequences of a fault have been pointed out, and a prayer in the end for God's assistance, will serve to give emphasis to the lesson in hand.

Helping to Spread the Faith

The First Commandment offers splendid opportunity to bring home to the children the duty of the Catholic layman to help spread the Faith. If they are deeply impressed with the fact that our Faith is the most precious treasure we possess, then they will surely want to do all in their power to make that Faith known to others. Most children take a very active part in foreign-mission work and delight in doing their bit for the spread of the Faith in other lands. They should also know something about the great Catholic lay organizations in our own and other countries; such as the National Council of Catholic Men, the National Council of Catholic Women, the Catholic Truth Society, the Central Verein, and others, and should be encouraged to bring in reports of the work being done by these bodies. In this way they will be better prepared to join the ranks of lay apostles when the time is ripe.

Use of the Bulletin Board

The work done by the discussion group should be supplemented by stories, dramatizations, and interesting and instructive articles placed on the bulletin board. Here it is that the Catholic Press should come in for its share of attention. The Catholic newspapers and magazines are full of items pertaining to Catholic life and action. Just a few items of recent date have been selected for mention here. They are such as

9

pertain particularly to the commandment under consideration: "British Premier Takes Slating for Church Joke — Macdonald Witticism in Canada Hotly Resented by London Catholic Press." "Miss Hawks Hits Vulgar Cartoon on Lateran Pact — N.C.W.C. President Protests to Magazine Editor on Offensive Pictures. No More Cause for Complaint, He Says." —The Catholic Bulletin, St. Paul, Minn. "The 'Chain-Letter' Madness." "The Stupidity of Many Superstitions." — Truth.

Such articles as these bring the children to a closer realization of the fact that the lessons in the Catechism class are lessons of everyday life and not a thing apart. They will help them to apply these lessons in their daily experiences and to glory in the fact that they are a part of that great body of men and women whose Catholicity is not a thing to be put on when convenient, but part of their very flesh and blood.

Further Suggestions

A special day could be set apart for a program of stories, hymns, literary selection, etc., pertaining to the commandment studied. A few selections are submitted herewith, although there is a great deal of material available in almost any teacher's library. The Catechism lesson proper follows as a final summary of the conclusions that have been arrived at in the various discussions.

"I am the Lord thy God. Thou shalt not have strange gods before Me."

10

Problems for Discussion

1. Michael is at a meeting of his club and hears the boys ridiculing the Catholic Faith. He is the only Catholic present. Has he any obligations? He has attended the Catholic school for eight years, but now he does not seem able to find an answer to their questions. What, do you think, is the trouble?

2. Mildred finds a book which speaks against God and religion and causes her to doubt her Faith. She reads it secretly in order to find out, as she says, what others think about religion. Is she allowed to read such a book? Is anyone ever allowed to read such a book? Suppose a learned and holy priest would read it, would he be committing a sin? On what would that depend? What should Mildred do in regard to the doubts that enter her mind about her Faith?

3. You are offered work as a clerk in a drug store, provided you are not a Catholic. May you accept?

4. Bess loves her parents very much. They have been very good to her and have given her everything she desired. At school she learns that she must love God more than anyone else. She is troubled because she believes she loves her parents more than God. She asks you about it. Can you help her?

5. You find a poor man alone in a hut. He is very ill and you advise him to make his peace with God. He tells you that his sins are too great to be forgiven. What sin does he commit by entertaining such thoughts? What would you tell him? Could you give

him an example of great sinners who were forgiven by God because they repented sincerely?

6. Your parents attend a funeral service at a Protestant church and wish you to go along. May Catholics attend such services? Would they be allowed to attend any Protestant services? Catholics are eager to have Protestants come to their church; why should they not return the courtesy?

7. A young man is leading a very sinful life. He realizes that he should change his ways and make his peace with God, but he always tells himself that there will be time enough tomorrow. What sin does he commit?

8. Mary is in serious trouble and becomes discouraged. She wishes that she would die. May she entertain such a wish? May people ever wish to die? Under what circumstances?

9. Henry and George are walking along the street when they suddenly meet with a gang of rough boys. The boys stop them and ask them whether they are Catholic. Must the two tell them? What is the reason for your answer?

10. Mr. Hill, a Catholic, is at a hotel with some of his friends. It is Friday and they all order meat for dinner. May Mr. Hill eat of the meat? Suppose Mr. Hill does not bless himself before meals, because he is ashamed to do so, does he commit a sin? Explain.

11. Sue and Jane go to the fortune teller "just for fun!" The fortune teller tells Sue something which

really comes to pass shortly afterwards. Sue asks you what you think about it. What would you tell her? Did the girls do right by going to a fortune teller?

12. Jack never went to any other but a good Catholic school. He seemed to be a good boy, but shortly after he went to work he lost his Faith. What, do you think, might have been the cause?

13. Someone sends you a chain prayer and tells you that you will be visited by some terrible calamity if you do not say it and help to circulate it. What should you do about it? What sin do you commit by believing in such things? Mention other superstitions you know about.

14. A neighbor of yours tells you that he went to the spiritualist and there spoke to his dead wife. Do you think that possible? How could such a thing happen? Do magicians practice their art through supernatural means, ordinarily? Would you be allowed to see a magician perform? Do you know that there is a Jesuit Father (Father Heredia) who can perform nearly all of the tricks which are done by the greatest magicians and even by would-be spiritualists? Is a Catholic allowed to consult a spiritualistic medium? Why not, if he does not believe in him?

15. Catherine takes her Protestant friend to church with her. They kneel before the statue of the Little Flower to pray. Ellen, Catherine's friend, asks whether the saint could really hear her, since it was only a statue after all. What shall Catherine tell her?

Ellen's mother says that Catholics do wrong to adore statues. What do you say?

16. You have a rosary that was blessed by the Holy Father. It is valued at 50 cents, but a friend offers you $5 on account of the blessings it bears. May you accept the money for the rosary? May you accept any money? May you give it to your friend as a gift?

17. Louis wears a four-leaved clover for good luck. You laugh at him, but he says you are just as bad, for you wear a medal and believe it is going to keep away all harm. How will you explain the difference?

18. A thief steals some money from church. Later he repents. In confessing his thefts, must he make any distinction between what he took from church and what he stole elsewhere? Suppose the money he took from church amounted to very little? What do we call such a sin? What other sins are called sacrileges?

19. John's mother advises him not to go with certain companions because they are harmful to him. He tells her not to worry, for he knows how to take care of himself and will not follow their bad example. Is John right?

The Teacher's Outline

We Worship God

By Faith:

1. Firm belief in God and His Word.
2. Learning what God has taught.
3. Professing our belief.

By Hope:

1. Unshaken trust in God.

14

2. Making acts of hope.
3. Proving our confidence by prayer and resignation.

By Charity:
   1. Sincere love of God.
   2. True love of our neighbor.
   3. Doing all for God by purity of intention.
   4. Suffering all rather than offend God.

By Religion:
   1. Sacrifice: the highest form of worship.
   2. Adoration: the occupation of the angels.
   3. Prayer: vow, praise, etc.
   4. Public Service, in church.

Sins Against Faith

All False Religions:
   1. Every religion, except that established by Christ.
   2. The maxim "all religions are equal" is false.
   3. The Catholic Church always persecuted.
      a) Persecutions of the early ages.
      b) Persecutions of the Reformation.
      c) Persecutions in all ages and every country.

Doubt:
   1. Doubt is hesitation to accept some dogma of faith.
   2. Involuntary, or put aside.
      a) Is not sinful.
      b) Is even meritorious.
      c) Many saints subject to it.
   3. Willful; i.e., deliberately entertained, is sinful, because:
      a) Implying that some dogma may be false.
      b) The Church may err in her teaching; and
      c) It may lead to a denial of the faith.
   4. To overcome such doubts:
      a) Make a direct act of the contrary virtue; as an act of faith.

b) Beg God's assistance.

c) Consult a wise confessor.

d) Avoid indiscreet discussions and arguments.

Disbelief:

Refusal to give assent to a revealed truth.

Denial:

External manifestations of disbelief, real or feigned, by words or deed.

Ignorance of Doctrines of the Church:

Ignorance of religion leads to many sins and errors, hence:

a) The necessity of catechism and instruction.

b) The responsibility of parents in regard to children.

c) The need of self-examination.

Neglect of Spiritual Duties:

1. As a knife rusts, if not used, so the faith dies, if not exercised.
2. The sacraments, sources of grace.
3. Mass on Sundays, etc., gives homage to God.
4. Morning and night prayers give daily strength.
5. Sermons and instructions revive faith and fervor.

Reading Bad Books:

1. Books against religion.
2. Books against morality.

Going to Non-Catholic Schools:

Taking Part in Services or Prayers of a False Religion:

Sins Against Hope

Despair:

1. Distrust of obtaining salvation and the means to it.
2. Guilty of despair:
   a) Who give up hope of salvation.
   b) Who, on account of their sins, reject the hope of pardon.

  c) Who, from experience of past weakness, cease to restrain their passions.

  d) Who, in sickness or adversity, wish for death.

  e) Who use unlawful means to procure relief.

  f) Who, if their prayer be not heard at once, fail to continue it.

 3. Remedies against despair:

  a) Meditate deeply on the mercy, love, and power of God.

  b) Pray God to strengthen your hope.

  c) Make frequent acts of hope.

  d) Invoke Mary, the refuge of sinners.

Presumption:

 1. Rash expectation of salvation, without taking the means to it.

 2. Guilty of presumption are they who:

  a) Continue in sin, hoping for deathbed repentance.

  b) Rely for salvation on prayer without repentance.

  c) Trust to their own strength to overcome temptation.

  d) Expose themselves to occasions of sin.

  e) In worldly matters trust to their own prudence only.

  f) Hope for a happy death without leading a good life.

False Worship

Superstitious Practices:

 1. Practices having no natural or supernatural connection with the end in view.

 2. Even religious things may be made subject to superstition.

 3. Kinds of superstitious practices:

  a) Consulting spiritualists.

  b) Consulting fortune tellers.

  c) Trusting to charms.

  d) Believing in omens.

  e) Believing in dreams.

Sacrilege:

1. Violation or irreverent treatment of what is consecrated to God.

Simony:

1. Buying or selling spiritual things for temporal price or reward.

Divine Honor Forbidden to Angels and Saints:

To them is due inferior worship only.

How We Must Honor the Saints:

1. By imitating their virtues according to our circumstances.
2. By celebrating their festivals.
3. By reading and making known their lives.
4. By joining confraternities under their invocation.
5. By visiting their shrines.
6. By adorning their altars.
7. By raising churches or altars to their honor.

Whom We Must Honor Especially:

1. The Blessed Virgin, Queen of Angels and of Men.
2. St. Joseph, Patron of the Universal Church.
3. Our Guardian Angels, to whom we owe reverence, love, and confidence.
4. The Patron Saints whose names we bear.
5. Special Saints under special circumstances.

We Owe Relative Honor (not for their own sakes) To:

1. Relics.
2. Crucifixes.
3. Holy Pictures.

Social Advantages of the First Commandment:

1. To this commandment we owe our superiority over pagan nations.
2. The observance of this commandment delivers us from such idolatries as those of the French Revolution.

3. Take away this commandment of the love of God and love of self alone remains.

4. Take away this commandment and man is degraded, regarding riches and pleasures as the sole objects of affection.

5. Take away this commandment and men, failing by these pleasures to satisfy their hearts, are driven to suicide.

6. Take away this commandment and the spirit of self-sacrifice is destroyed, by which human nature is ennobled, and on which society thrives and prospers.[1]

Scripture Texts

He that loveth danger shall perish in it. *Ecclus.* iii. 27.

Beware of false prophets. *Matt.* vii. 15.

I desire not the death of the wicked. *Ezech.* xxxiii. 11.

If your sins be as scarlet, they shall be made white as snow. *Isa.* i. 18.

Depart into everlasting fire. *Matt.* xxv. 41.

Delay not to be converted: defer it not from day to day. *Ecclus.* v. 8.

Not every one that saith to Me Lord, Lord, shall enter into the kingdom of heaven. *Matt.* vii. 21.

That old serpent who seduceth the whole world. *Apoc.* xii. 9.

Cursed be the man that maketh a graven thing. *Deut.* xxvii. 15.

Let them be all confounded that adore graven things. *Ps.* xcvi. 7.

The wickedness of idols is the beginning and end of all evil. *Wisd.* xiv. 27.

If God be for us, who is against us? *Rom.* viii. 31.

---

[1]Outline according to Howe.

He that dwelleth in the aid of the Most High shall abide under the protection of God. *Ps.* xc. 1.

Neither let there be found among you any one that . . . observeth dreams or omens . . . nor any one that consulteth fortune tellers. *Deut.* xviii. 10, 11.

To them that love God all things work together unto good. *Rom.* viii. 28.

You shall not divine, nor observe dreams. *Lev.* xix. 26.

Dreams follow many cares. *Eccles.* v. 2.

Dreams have deceived many, and they have failed to put their trust in them. *Ecclus.* xxxiv. 7.

Touch ye not My annointed, and do no evil to My prophets. *Ps.* civ. 15.

Fear the Lord and reverence His priests. *Ecclus.* vii. 13.

Reverence My sanctuary. *Lev.* xix. 30.

If any man violate the Temple of God, him shall God destroy. *I Cor.* iii. 17.

They shall not touch the vessels of the sanctuary. *Num.* iv. 15.

Stories to Be Looked Up and Related by the Children

Story of St. Germaine (faith, hope, charity).
St. Mary Magdalen (hope).
Story of the Good Thief (hope).
Story of Judas Iscariot (despair).
Story of St. Peter's denial and forgiveness (hope).
Parable of the Prodigal Son.
Parable of the Lost Sheep.
Saints who died for their faith, especially children's own patron saints.
Blessed Thomas More and Blessed John Fisher.

St. Monica.
St. Martina, January 30.
St. Eustachius, September 20.
St. Lucy, December 13.
St. Lawrence.
Simon Magnus.
Jeroboam Seizing the Prophet, *III Kings* xiii. 4.
St. Thomas, the Apostle.
Mary Murmuring against Moses. *Num.* xii. 10.
Story of the Patient Job.
St. Peter Released from Prison.
Baltassar Seizing the Sacred Vessels.
History of the Druids.
Story of the Theban Legion.

Picture Studies

The Good Shepherd, Plockhorst.
St. Peter on the Waves, Plockhorst.
Guardian Angel, Plockhorst.
Adoration of the Magi, Leinweber.
St. Stephen, Martyr, Leinweber.
St. Peter's Deliverance from Prison, Leinweber.
Peter Denies Christ, Leinweber.
Jesus Walking on the Sea, Leinweber.
Jesus Purgeth the Temple, Leinweber.
The Prodigal Son, Leinweber.
Other artists whose Biblical pictures are well worth studying are: Feuerstein, Hoffmann, Untersberger.

Hymns

Blest is the Faith, Father Faber, in St. Gregory Hymnal.
Faith of Our Fathers, Father Faber, in St. Gregory Hymnal.
Thee Will I Love, My Dearest Treasure, Bonvin.
Hymns to various patron saints.

Some Short Stories[1]

The Fatal Picture

Philip, king of the Franks, heard that it was prophesied that if he destroyed a certain picture his death would immediately follow. To show his contempt for such superstitious sayings, he had the picture in question brought to him, and with his own hand flung it into the fire. Nothing happened to him, we need hardly say, and the superstitious people were quite out of countenance. — *Spirago.*

The Man Who Believeth Nothing, and Yet Believed What No One Else Believed

A priest was returning with several other persons from a pilgrimage by train. A stranger entered and took a vacant place in the railway carriage occupied by the party of pilgrims. When he saw who were his traveling companions, and noticed the rosaries in their hands, he could not refrain from making some contemptuous remarks concerning their credulity, as he termed their faith, ending by saying in a boastful manner: "As for me, I believe in nothing." "Pardon me, sir," the priest rejoined, "you believe a great deal. In one respect you believe more than any of us do." The gentleman expressed the wish to be told what was meant; how, he asked, did he believe what they

[1] A group of distinctively modern instances should supplement this list. — *Editor.*

did not? For some time he had to wait for an answer; but as he would not be refused, and declared that he should not take offense, whatever was said, the priest at length replied: "My dear sir, you believe that you are a very clever fellow. I can assure you that none of us believe that." All the people present laughed heartily; the unfortunate man colored painfully and changed coaches at the next station. — *Spirago.*

Victim of a Fortune Teller

A young man was one day present while a fortune teller was plying her trade, and was ridiculing her pretensions to tell the future. To avenge herself, she told him he would die within the year, and that, too, in September. The young man laughed at first, but as it was personal, he began shortly to think of it seriously, and spoke to his parents of it. These took the common-sense view of the matter, and explained how the prediction could mean nothing, the old witch merely desiring to frighten him for his having laughed at her. The boy felt the force of all this, yet could not shake off the thought of a fatal prediction; night and day it haunted him, till at length he became ill, and his very life was in danger. On September 30, he was extremely low, so that the doctor thought he could hardly recover. "If, however," he continued, "he gets over tonight, he is safe. It is fear that is killing him." His parents and friends had a most anxious time of it. At length, however, the clock struck midnight. September was gone, October was in, and the young man coming round to himself, exclaimed: "Thank God, He has preserved me to you yet awhile. Ask Him to forgive my folly." In matters of faith we must be simple-minded and humble; at the same time we should be strong and determined in rejecting superstition. — *Urban.*

A Bad Dream

A certain business man came into great straits. He complained bitterly about his misery. His entire life became distasteful to him. But his wife had a pious, Christian mind and heart; therefore she tried to console her husband and to cheer him up. But all was in vain. Once this woman, too, sat there sad and disconsolate and did not want even to eat. Her husband asked her what the trouble was. At first his wife did not want to answer at all. Finally she said: "Last night I dreamed that our Blessed Lord had died and all the angels went along with the funeral and wept most bitterly. That almost broke my heart, and I am still very sad over it." "Nonsense!" said her husband. "Can God die?" Then the face of this woman became cheerful again, and looking kindly into the eyes of her husband, she said: "Therefore He still lives, the good God?" "Yes, of course God still lives; how can you talk so childishly?" Then the woman said very seriously: "But if the good God still lives, why have you no longer any confidence in Him?" Thereupon this man's eyes were opened again and he said: "Yes, dear wife, you are right. You are more sensible and more Christian than I. From now on I will trust in God." — *Baierl.*

The Sea in a Little Hole

St. Augustine, one of the greatest doctors of the Church, was walking one day on the shore of the Mediterranean Sea. He was meditating on the Most Holy Trinity, and sought to fathom it, in order that he might be able to explain it the better in a work he was about to compose, or in sermons he might have to preach. He was absorbed in this inquiry, when he saw a little boy carrying water continually from the sea in a small shell, and throwing it into a hole which he had made in the sand. "What is that you are doing, my little boy?" said St. Augustine. "I am trying to put all the water of the sea in this little hole." "But, my dear child, that is impossible," resumed the holy bishop, laughing heartily at the child's artless simplicity; "do you not perceive that the hole is too small, and the sea too large?" "You think, then, that I shall not succeed? Well! I can assure you it will be easier for me to put all the water of the sea into this little hole, than for you to comprehend or explain the doctrine of the Holy Trinity." No sooner had the child spoken these words than he disappeared. It was an angel who had taken that form to give St. Augustine this important lesson. The learned doctor thanked God for such a favor, and gave himself no further trouble endeavoring to penetrate inscrutable mysteries. — *Catholic Gems and Pearls.*

A Bold General

When Frederick the Great of Prussia was ridiculing Christ and Christianity before a company of his nobles and generals, who were convulsed with laughter at the King's coarse witticisms, there was one brave general who remained gloomily silent. It was Joachim von Ziethen, one of the ablest and bravest generals there. Rising, at last, and shaking his gray head solemnly, he said to the King:

"Your majesty knows well that in war I have never feared any danger, and everywhere I have boldly risked my life for you and your country. But there is One above us Who is greater than you and I — greater than all men; He is the Savior and Redeemer, Who died also for your majesty, and has dearly bought us all with His own blood. This Holy One I can never allow to be mocked or insulted; for on Him repose my faith, my comfort, and my hope of life and death. In the power of this faith your brave army has courageously fought and conquered. If your majesty undermines this faith, you undermine at the same time the welfare of your state. I salute your majesty."

Frederick looked at the man in admiration, and then and there in the presence of the illustrious company, apologized to him for what he had said. — *Catholic Gems and Pearls.*

Selections

He who, from zone to zone,
  Guides through the boundless sky thy certain flight
In the long way that I must tread alone
  Will lead my steps aright.

— W. C. Bryant

If I met a priest and an angel, I would salute the priest
before saluting the angel.

— Curé d'Ars

Every day is a fresh beginning;
  Listen, my soul, to the glad refrain,
And, spite of old sorrow and older sinning,
  And puzzles forecasted and possible pain,
  Take heart with the day, and begin again.

Love thy God, and love Him only,
And thy breast will ne'er be lonely.
In that one great Spirit meet
All things mighty, grave and sweet.
Vainly strives the soul to mingle
With a being of our kind;
Vainly hearts with hearts are twined,
For the deepest still is single.
An impalpable resistance
Holds like natures at a distance.
Mortal! love that Holy One,
Or dwell for aye alone.

— Aubrey de Vere

Our hearts were made for Thee, O Lord,
  And restless must they be
Until — O Lord, this grace accord!
  Until they rest in Thee.

— St. Augustine

More things are wrought by prayer than this world
dreams of. — *Tennyson.*

> The year's at the Spring,
> And day's at the Morn;
> Morning's at seven;
> The hillside's dew-pearled;
> The lark's on the wing;
> The snail's on the thorn;
> God's in His heaven, —
> All's right with the world!
> — *Robert Browning*

A Child's Thought of God

They say that God lives very high;
But, if you look above the pines,
You cannot see our God; and why?

And, if you dig down in the mines,
You never see Him in the gold;
Though from Him all that's glory shines.

God is so good He wears a fold
Of heaven and earth across His face,
Like secrets kept for love, untold.

But still I feel that His embrace
Slide down by thrills through all things made —
Through sight and sound of every place.

As if my tender mother laid
On my shut lips her kisses' pressure,
Half waking me at night, and said
"Who kissed you through the dark, dear guesser?"
— *Mrs. Browning*

He Prayeth Best

Farewell, Farewell! But this I tell
To thee, thou wedding guest,
He prayeth well who loveth well,
Both man, and bird, and beast.

He prayeth best who loveth best,
All things both great and small,
For the dear Lord, who loveth us,
He made and loveth all.
— Samuel Taylor Coleridge

"God sees the little sparrow fall,
It meets His tender view;
If God so loves the little birds,
I know He loves me, too."

Heliogabalus and the Stone

Heliogabalus became Emperor of Rome, A.D. 218. He came from Syria, and brought with him a black stone of triangular form, which he adored as his god. He walked to and fro, and danced before it; a temple was built to receive it, and all the other gods of the empire had to yield it the place of honor.
— Roman History.

Pagan Worship

In the worship of idols, offerings were made to the gods, of meal or flour, mixed with salt, of libations of honey and incense. Not only animals, but even human beings were offered in sacrifice, and among the Chanaanites, especially, the children of the most noble families. It was thus the pagans served their gods.

Faith

O gift of gifts! O grace of Faith!
　My God, how can it be
That Thou, who hast discerning love,
　Should give that gift to me?

There was a place, there was a time,
　Whether by night or day,
Thy Spirit came and left that gift,
　And went upon His way.

How many hearts Thou mightst have had
　More innocent than mine,
How many souls more worthy far
　Of that sweet touch of Thine!

Ah grace! into unlikeliest hearts
　It is thy boast to come,
The glory of thy light to find
　In darkest spots a home.

How can they live, how will they die,
　How bear the cross of grief,
Who have not got the light of faith,
　The courage of belief?

The crowd of cares, the weightiest cross
　Seem trifles less than light;
Earth looks so little and so low,
　When faith shines full and bright.

Oh, happy, happy that I am!
　If thou canst be, O Faith,
The treasure that thou art in life,
　What wilt thou be in death?

Thy choice, O God of goodness! then
  I lovingly adore;
O give me grace to keep Thy grace,
  And grace to merit more.

                    — *Father Faber*

THE SECOND COMMANDMENT[1]

In this study of the Second Commandment, the plan of the Fourth Commandment in the October (1929) issue of the *Catholic School Journal* will be followed. Hence, such devices as the Bulletin Boards, Problems, Dramatization, will again be used at the teacher's discretion.

"Thou shalt not take the name of the Lord thy God in vain; for he shall not be unpunished that taketh His name upon a vain thing." *Deut.* v. 11.

These words of Holy Scripture will be written on the upper part of the blackboard during the time spent at the study of this commandment. Should more board space be available, the Scripture texts or the quotations found later in this study could be well used on the same.

The following pictures ought to be at hand, besides others to which the teacher has access or which she may prefer:

Adam and Eve Driven Out of Paradise—Doré
Jacob Blessing His Sons—Rembrandt
Moses Receiving the Tables of the Laws—Raphael
Moses Presenting Them to the People—Raphael
Angels Singing at the Nativity—Sinkel or Correggio

---

[1]For grades 5 and 6.

Sermon on the Mount—Bida
Jesus, Friend of Children—Plockhorst
Christ Before Pilate—Hoffman
His Blood be Upon Us and Our Children—Munkacsy
Denial of Peter—Harrach
Jesus Before the High Priest—Seifert
The Crucifixion (Blaspheming Christ)—Scene from Oberammergau
David—Michelangelo
Crusaders—
The Last Judgment—Michelangelo

Each of these pictures has a lesson involving some phase of the Second Commandment. The Spiritual Bulletin Board, as well as the others, are at the command of the pupils and the teachers for pictures, poems, slogans, and any original suggestions.

In the hands of the children will be Deharbe's Catechism and a Bible History as the required texts. As many additional sources as possible should be at the disposal of the children.

As frequently during the day as possible, the teacher will refer to the Second Commandment in a natural and opportune way. In the reading class she might select poems such as Faber's "Jesus, the very thought of Thee"; in the spelling class, such words as blasphemy, covenant, reverence, etc.

The hymn "The Second Commandment" by Katherine Bainbridge (M. Witmark and Sons, New York), will be appropriate; also the "Divine Praises" from any hymnal. To the usual prayers of the day, the little ejaculation, "Blessed be His Holy Name," can be added, and so again and again during these days the children will be reminded of their sacred obligations in reference to the Second Commandment.

Instruction Period

The period opens with a little prayer and a hymn. "Today we start our work on the study of the Second Commandment. We read in Holy Scripture how Moses ascended Mount Sinai while the Jews were praying at the foot of the mountain. Thunder began to be heard, and lightning to flash, and a very thick cloud to cover the mount, and the noise of the trumpet sounded exceedingly loud, and the people feared. *Exod*. xix. 16. And God said: Thou shalt not take the name of the Lord thy God in vain; for he shall not be unpunished that taketh His name upon a vain thing. *Deut*. v. 11. George, you have prepared this passage from Holy Writ, you will now read it to the class." George, who has prepared it well, will read it to the class to the best of his ability. He reads the entire chapter which gives the account of the giving of the Ten Commandments. *Exod*. xx. 1–25.

"What especially noteworthy do you see in this commandment which you do not meet with in any of the other commandments?" (It is the only commandment to which a punishment is attached.)

"Surely now, children, you realize better the awful responsibility of taking the name of God in vain. The Jews held the name "Jehova" in such awe and veneration, that never would they pronounce it. Even the High Priest was not permitted to say it oftener than once a year, and that on the solemn Feast of the Atonement. Instead of the word, Jehova, they called God, Adonai. God's awful majesty and perfection, immense knowledge, boundless wisdom, sanctity, and justice are just as sacred today as they were in the days when He gave the solemn order, 'Thou shalt not take the Name of God in vain.' You want to know all that God demands of you in His Second Commandment in order that you may never offend Him through any violation of the same, but rather that you may honor Him all your life by faithfully keeping it."

The teacher then briefly outlines the work, tries to arouse enthusiasm and happy coöperation. She will try especially to have the children present their own problems at the appointed recitation periods. All the problems and stories will deal with the five major points in the Second Commandment as follows: (1) Reverence for the Holy Name of God as opposed to profanation; (2) Speaking with reverence of religion as opposed to deriding religion; (3) Oaths, good and bad; swearing; (4) Blasphemy and cursing; (5) Vows.

"For tomorrow's lesson you will all tell a story which refers to this commandment. Select them from the Bible History. I know you will all be eager to show how God rewards the faithful observance of His law and punishes the violation of it."

As much freedom as possible should be given the

children in the selection of their stories, both Biblical and otherwise, just so they are pertinent to the work at hand.

Children's Stories in Class

The children, in a socialized recitation, will tell their stories to the class. Should discussions arise, so much the better, because it is through these personal revelations that the alert teacher will find an unlimited source of material for character training.

Bible History Stories

The Promise of a Redeemer.
The Primal Curse.
God's Covenant After the Deluge.
Noah's Curse Upon Cham.
Jacob Blessing His Sons.
The Patience of Job.
Pharaoh's Punishment for Not Keeping His Word.
The Ten Commandments Given to Moses 'midst Thunder and Lightning.
Core, Dathan, Abiron.
The Reverence Shown the Ark of the Covenant.
David and the Psalms.
Magnificence of the Vessels, etc., Used in the Temple.
Sennacherib.
Naboth, King Achab, Queen Jezabel.
Leprosy Attacks Ozias for Daring to Strike the High Priest.
Susanna.
Eliseus and the Bears.
The Prophet Isaias, Who Looked into Heaven and Heard the Hymn: Holy, Holy, Holy.
The Blessed Virgin: "Behold from Henceforth All Generations Shall Call Me Blessed."

Angels' Hymn at the Nativity: "Glory to God in the Highest."
Simeon's Reverence for the Infant Jesus.
The Sermon on the Mount. The Passage, "Swear Not . . ."
The Oath of Herod.
Christ Conferring the Primacy on Peter. "Whatsoever . . ."
Jesus and the Children. Scandal Punished.
The Lord's Prayer: "Hallowed be Thy Name."
Jesus Entering Jerusalem: "Hosanna to the Son of David."
Jesus Before Pilate.
Jesus Before the High Priest.
The Denial of Peter.
The Insults Heaped Upon Christ at the Scourging and the
    Crowning with Thorns.
"His Blood be Upon Us and Our Children."
The Blasphemies at the Crucifixion and Those of the
    Wicked Thief.

All the stories need not be told "en masse," but, perhaps, as the problems would suggest one or the other, they would become more effective.

Stories of the Saints

Any of the Martyrs Who Preferred Death to the Violation
    of Their Baptismal Vows.
St. Charles Borromeo.
St. Mamertus; the Rogation Days.
St. Aloysius, Who Grieved All His Life for Using Profane
    Words Once When a Child.
St. Paul, Who Uses the Holy Name of Jesus Most Frequently.
St. Francis of Assisi.
Louis of Thuringia and His Wife, St. Elizabeth.
St. Frances of Rome.
St. Augustine.
St. Stanislaus Kostka.
St. John Capistran.
St. Thais, Never Pronounced the Name of God, "O Thou,
    Who Hast Made Me."

St. Alphonsus.

St. Teresa the Great.

St. Jane Frances de Chantal.

St. Eligeus.

Other Stories

Julian the Apostate. "Galilean, Thou Has Conquered!"

King Clovis Vows to Become a Christian.

Luther's Vow.

Vows of the Crusaders: Godfrey, Richard, Barbarossa, Philip, Louis.

Religious Vows.

Oberammergau Vow.

Alexander of Macedonia; Met the High Priest in His Priestly Robes and Knelt Before Him. "Not to Him Have I Bowed My Knee, But to the Lord God Whose Priest He Is."

The Old Man and the Crucifix; in Baierl, page 134.

King Arthur Stories.

Sir Thomas More.

Regulus, the Roman General in Carthage.

Nestorius Punished Because He Refused the Title, Mother of God, to Mary.

Respect Shown by Newton to the Holy Name.

The Priest and His Guardian Angel.

Voltaire.

A Mother's Curse.

Washington, Lincoln, Roosevelt (Found in the Holy Name pamphlet).

No doubt, the children themselves will know many stories based upon the keeping of a promise or the taking of God's Name in vain. Also soldier stories and their loyalty to their oath will be very instructive. The bibliography will give the names of the books from which most of the above stories were selected.

38

Problems

The following problems, and many others with which the teacher has come in contact, are offered; as well as those which the children will be eager to present. When possible, the teacher will have a short outline at the board referring to the day's problems. This outline can be made in class with the suggestions of the pupils. Let the teacher realize that through such free discussions of problems, she can make the lessons, learned in the schoolrooms, function most effectively in their daily lives and so draw the souls of her children closer to the great Friend of children. Surely a serious discussion of a problem can never be a loss of time.

Problems of School and Playground

1. During the day, so often, children, you think of your parents, your home, the baseball game. How often do you think of Jesus? Your mother loves you when you say, "Mother, dear," and such loving words sincerely. Wouldn't Jesus love you much, too, if during the day you would often say to Him: "Jesus, Jesus." How often do you think you could easily do so? Try it this day at every change of lessons.

2. How could you show reverence to the Holy Name of Jesus? (Bowing my head slightly when it is pronounced, taking off my hat, never using it vainly.)

3. What would you say to a boy if you heard him use the word "Jesus" in anger?

4. What do you think of a child who laughs upon hearing another child say the name of God in an angry or irreverential tone? Which child, do you think, has committed the graver sin?

5. You are a young boy. You hear one of the big boys

39

using very bad language and often saying the Holy Names in a shocking way. Would you let him talk like that, or would you have courage enough to tell him not to speak so. Tell the class what you would really say to him.

6. What do you think of telling your teacher that a certain child often uses the name of Jesus irreverently or curses and swears? Do you think you are obliged to tell?

7. How would you make good the wrong you have done by using the name of God in anger before a group of children? (Confession and apology publicly given.)

8. The priest has given the order that the next one he hears cursing on the playground will be expelled. You hear a boy, who always used bad language when no teacher or priest is near, do so. What would you do or say to him?

9. Do you think cursing on the part of a Catholic child a bigger sin against God than if he were a Protestant? Why? (A Catholic should know better.)

10. A boy thinks it is smart to imitate the bad language he hears from grown-up people. He shows off before his friends through cursing. What kind of sin do you think he is committing and how many?

11. You have found a newspaper like the Menace on your way to school. You know it contains lies and insults to the Catholic Priest, Sister, and Religion. What will you do with that paper?

12. A person started to use bad words and curses at the age of 10 years. He does it, let us say, ten times a day. (Some people, who have formed the habit, do it much oftener.) He does this until he is 60 years old. Just figure out how many times he has offended God in his wicked life. (182,500.) How could you make reparation to some degree for the terrible wrong he has done God?

13. Many children are in purgatory for using bad words on the playground and so teaching them to others. If they could

come back to their play, what do you imagine they would say and do now?

14. Why should such expressions as "Cross my heart, I'm telling the truth," and "Sure as heaven," even though they are not sins, very seldom be used?

15. What is the best act of reparation to God you could make when you hear someone using His Name in vain? (Pronounce the name devoutly, make an act of sorrow for him.)

16. What beautiful habit could you learn to form now when you hear bad language? (Say "Jesus Christ" most devoutly when you hear it the other way.)

17. How could a group of boys prevent one or more boys from using the Holy Names profanely or from using vulgar expressions on the playground, without telling the teacher on them?

18. A little boy or girl has come to school with the evil habit we are discussing. The parents thought it "cute" when the little one would use these words. How could the children at school help the child to break this habit without offending the parents?

19. How would you act toward a child who is trying to overcome his vicious habit, but who very often does forget himself?

20. Don't forget, dear children, that Jesus rests upon your tongue in Holy Communion. Can He be pleased to rest on a tongue that curses and uses His Holy Name or that of His Mother so irreverently?

Problems at Home

1. Why do you think the language of the home can so easily be judged by that of the children? Therefore, what do you think to be a very important obligation of any father and mother?

2. Would you want your home to be judged by the language

you are using? If not, why not? And what will you do about it?

3. Should your father at times say very unbecoming and even sinful words, could you tell him it is wrong and you do not like it? If he gets angry with you for telling him, could you show him some other way that you don't want him to talk like that?

4. The parents often use such bad language so much, that they do not realize anymore they are doing it. What could be done in such a family to protect the children?

5. I know of a certain child who was purposely taught to curse by another person. The parents are much grieved, but again and again the child will forget himself. What do you think of the guilt of the person who is responsible?

6. A little boy has followed the example of his father in cursing. When the mother corrects him, he says: "Daddy does it, why can't I?" What do you think that mother ought to do?

7. If a person has done much swearing and cursing so that he now is in the habit of doing it, what kind of sin is he committing when he does it even without his realizing it?

8. A family consists of parents and three children, age 10, 8, 4. The father is a Protestant and is very bitter toward the Catholic school and Church. He is becoming more bitter day by day because the children must attend the Catholic school. In every way possible he scoffs at the Priest, the Sisters, Confession, Communion. All the poor mother can do is to keep quiet and to try to keep the children good. What life lesson can you learn from this?

9. Some men so readily curse their horses, or cars, or what not. What do you think of such ingratitude to God?

10. What can you do in your own families, even though you are quite young, and even though your family never uses coarse and sinful language, to raise its moral standard still higher in reference to the Second Commandment?

Problems for Later Life

(Some of these problems might refer even to the present age of the children.) Suggested outlines for the blackboard or bulletin board:

Profanation

1. Speak with reverence of God:
   Lord, Jesus Christ, Holy Trinity.
2. Not use the name of God in vain:
   a) Mortal sin if deliberately irreverential and contemptuous;*
   b) Venial if not so, if in mere ordinary use.
3. Speak with reverence of Holy Persons and Holy Things: Saints, Angels, Priests, Religious, Mass, Sacraments.
4. Profane words:
   a) Unbecoming words: hell, devil, etc.;
   b) Guilt — usually venial; however, it depends upon the irreverence and the scandal.

Problems

1. You are a graduate of a Catholic high school or college. Would this fact add to the seriousness of the sin you commit by using the name of God in vain, especially in the presence of non-Catholics?

2. What do you think a good Catholic young person would do, should he find that his friends, time and again, use profane language or speak deridingly of holy things?

3. Some young men commonly indulge in (as one writer puts it) "deviled" language. They frequently use words that refer to hell, satan; this is often called "swearing," but it is only vulgar. Although these words in themselves are not sin-

---

*These Outlines are all based upon *The Catechist*, by Very Rev. Canon Howe. The notes under "Guilt, Venial or Mortal," in all cases are quoted from Father Howe's *The Second Commandment*, pp. 405–419.

ful, what about the scandal given to bystanders and especially to children?

4. When will profanity amount to a mortal sin? The real test is supplied by St. Thomas: "In sinful words what has chiefly to be noticed is the spirit (disposition of mind) in which they are uttered."

5. What do you say about using the words of Holy Scripture irreverently?

Deriding Religion

1. What would you do in a group if practically everyone is deriding what you hold sacred; e.g., the confessional, holy water. Would you be obliged to object?

2. Very often Catholics themselves, by their very free and jocose way of speaking, are the cause of others deriding religion. What should these Catholics do to overcome their habit?

3. What do you think of a magazine which will permit cartoons that put some one or other teaching of the Church or some member of the clergy, perhaps the Pope, in a ridiculous light? If you are subscribing to such a magazine and in general it is a good paper, what will you do?

4. Catholics often, by their stupidity, bring the scorn of others upon the Church. How should a Catholic continue to educate himself, or has he done enough when he has made his Solemn Communion?

5. What do you think of the Holy Name Society?

Blasphemy

1. Definition: Blasphemy is any word, thought, desire, act, insulting to God.

2. Direct: (a) Denying the attributes of God. (b) Attributing imperfections to God. (c) Speaking with contempt of God.

3. Indirect: Against the Blessed Virgin, the saints, or holy things.

4. Guilt: Mortal sin, in itself, or when it is a habit unregretted. Venial sin, if without full advertence, or without scandal.

Problems

1. Why are such expressions as "God is cruel, unjust; God doesn't care for me; What good is praying anyway?" etc., in time of trial or sorrow, so grievously sinful?

2. If any expressions like the above are made without due deliberation, and the person is immediately sorry, what do you think of the sin?

3. Should you be in the presence of a fallen-away Catholic who sneers at a Priest, the Sacraments, and even at God, what would you do?

4. What about such acts as desecrating a church or a crucifix out of sheer contempt?

5. How could you commit a sin of blasphemy by thought? What kind of sin would it be?

Cursing

1. Definition: Cursing is wishing evil upon oneself or upon God's creatures.
2. Directly opposed to Charity.
3. Gives bad example.
4. The language of hell.
5. Scripture gives four cases in which God hears curses:
    a) Poor cursing the rich who oppress them.
    b) Widows and orphans cursing their oppressors.
    c) Parents cursing their children.
    d) People cursing themselves.
6. Guilt:
    Mortal when the evil wished is grievous.
    Venial when the evil wished is not grievous.

Oaths

1. Definition:
   An oath is calling God to witness the truth of what we say. Same as to swear.
2. Lawful Oath:
   a) Truth; Judgment, that is with reflection, discretion, good cause.
   b) Certain conditions make necessary the taking of an oath.
3. False Oaths (Perjury):
   a) Wanting in truthfulness.
   b) Most grievous sin, even if the lie is trifling.
4. Rash Oaths:
   a) Wanting in judgment, thought, reflection.
   b) Usually venial, unless there be danger of perjury or scandal.
5. Unjust Oath:
   a) To do something sinful.
   b) Mortal sin against the sanctity of God.
6. Unnecessary Oath:
   a) Swearing without sufficient cause.
   b) Not usually grievous, yet displeasing to God.

Problems

1. You are called upon the witness stand. Your own good name will be tarnished and perhaps your money lost if you tell the whole truth about the defendant, who is your business partner, your relative, or your friend. You have sworn "To tell the truth, the whole truth, and nothing but the truth; so Help me God!" Regardless of your loss, what must you do?

2. On the witness stand you have become all muddled in a cross-examination. You tell an untruth. Have you committed perjury?

3. A man swears never to forgive his wayward son or daughter. What do you know about such an oath?

46

4. Why does the Church forbid secret societies like the Free Masons?

5. Such expressions as "God knows, God is my witness, Before God," can be oaths or not. What does this depend upon? (Intention of both parties.) Why should you avoid such strong language as "I swear," or "Upon my soul!" even though they do not mean an oath?

Vows

1. Definition:
   a) A vow is a promise to God, binding oneself to do some good.
   b) It must be a true promise, have deliberation, such as is necessary for a mortal sin; made to God; with knowledge and liberty.
   c) Guilt: mortal or venial, as it is of greater or less moment.
2. Examples of vows.

Problems

1. What do you think of a person who does not keep even his simple promises? What effect would continually breaking your word have upon your character?

2. A girl 12 years old became mortally sick. She promised to consecrate her life to God should she recover. This was some years ago. She recovered but has not kept her promise. What have you to say about this?

3. Even the saints as a rule did not take a vow without the consent of their confessor. Why should this not be done secretly?

4. A man frequently misses Mass on Sundays. Do you think, for the sake of forcing himself to it, he might make a vow never again to miss Mass on Sundays?

5. Your father makes a promise to build an altar for the church. He dies suddenly. Are you, as his heir, bound to keep the solemn promise and to donate the altar?

6. Why cannot a Catholic who is duly married get a divorce and remarry? (The marriage *vows* are indissoluble.)

7. If Vows are such serious things, why should anybody ever make them?

Holy Name Society

The above problems will take a number of days. After this, one good recitation period would be most profitably spent in the study of the Organization and the Ideals of the Holy Name Society. The teacher may secure material from The National Headquarters of the Holy Name Society, 884 Lexington Ave., New York City. This may be given the pupils who will recite to the class on special topics selected.

Dramatization

Children of all ages love to dramatize. The story of Job, who blessed the Lord in trials, or any of the above stories can easily be dramatized. The Psalms of David might be presented in pantomime, a reader giving the Psalms from the side.

Drill and Summary

True-False Test

The next recitation will have for its aim the final drill of the Catechism questions. This will be followed by the *Objective Test*.

Write the word true or false in the lines at the end of each statement, making the statement correct.

1. Every sin against the Second Commandment is a mortal sin . . . .

2. You are obliged to tell an older person that he has no right to use curse words as he does ....

3. Perjury or the taking of a false oath is always a mortal sin ....

4. The Second Commandment is the only one accompanied with a threat ....

5. A vow that a child makes does not bind him when he is grown up ....

6. If you have taken a false oath, thereby causing another to lose his good name, you must admit publicly that your oath was false ....

7. If a man curses through a habit which he is trying to overcome, he is committing a venial sin ....

8. If you prevent another from committing a sin against the Commandment, God will give you a special reward ....

9. A little boy or girl can do much to prevent bad language on the playground ....

10. On your playground, much bad language is being used ....

Best Answer

1. I must keep my good promises because:
   a) It is always a sin not to keep them.
   b) The breaking of them will weaken me morally.
   c) I will lose my good name.
2. I will never use the Name of God in vain because:
   a) The Second Commandment forbids it.
   b) Otherwise my parents will punish me.
3. I will join the Holy Name Society sometime because:
   a) It pledges me to use God's name reverently.
   b) The other boys belong to it.
   c) The society always has a summer outing.
4. When I hear some other boy or girl curse:
   a) I will run away.
   b) I will laugh.
   c) I will tell him or her how wrong it is.

5. When I have used a bad word before little sister:
   a) I will ask her not to tell on me.
   b) I will pretend I did not say it.
   c) I will tell her I am sorry that I was naughty and offended God.

Fill in the Blanks

The Second Commandment deals especially with the five following points:

. . . .

. . . .

Name ten Bible History stories or name the people in these stories relative to the Second Commandment:

. . . .

Class Projects

The children will make a special effort to watch their own speech and that of their companions during these weeks and correct them on every occasion necessary.

Should the Holy Name Society (Junior Branch) be in existence in the school, a Junior Holy Name Rally could be held.

Notebooks of poems, slogans, memory gems, gathered by the children, could be displayed for the benefit of the other classes.

A very beautiful close to the study of this commandment, would be a General Holy Communion in Reparation for the blasphemies offered to God.

Finally, the movie "The Blasphemer," by the Catholic Dramatic Art Society, could be given for the children and for the parish.

(In any of the above projects, if the permission of the pastor is necessary, it must be secured first.)

Books of Stories

Teachers' Handbook to the Catechism, Vol. II, Rev. A. Urban, pp. 237–241.

Explanation of the Commandments, Rev. H. Rolfus, pp. 119–135.

Bible History, Benziger.

High School Catechism, Msgr. P. Stockman, pp. 643–646.

Anecdotes and Examples for the Catechist. Spirago and Baxter.

The Catechism Explained, J. J. Baierl, pp. 124–162.

Special References:

The Catechist, Vol. I, Very Rev. Canon Howe, Benziger Bros.

Catechetical Methods, Rev. R. G, Bandas, Joseph F. Wagner, Inc., New York, N. Y.

BIBLICAL REFERENCES

Who is like to Thee, among the strong, O Lord? who is like to Thee, glorious in holiness, terrible and praiseworthy, doing wonders? *Exod.* xv. 11.

Thou shalt not take the name of the Lord thy God in vain; for the Lord will not hold him guiltless that shall take the name of the Lord his God in vain. *Exod.* xx. 7.

Thou shalt fear the Lord thy God and shalt serve Him only, and thou shalt swear by His name. *Deut.* vi. 13.

And looking back, he saw them, and cursed them in the name of the Lord: and there came forth two bears out of the forest, and tore of them two and forty boys. *IV Kings* ii. 24.

And he loved cursing, and it shall come unto him: and he would not have blessing, and it shall be far from him. *Ps.* cviii. 18.

All His commandments are faithful: confirmed for ever and ever, made in truth and equity. *Ps.* cx. 8.

Holy and terrible is His Name. *Ps.* cx. 9.

The fear of the Lord is the beginning of wisdom. *Ps.* cx. 10.

But I say unto you, not to swear at all, neither by heaven for it is the throne of God. *Matt.* v. 34.

But I say unto you, that every idle word that men shall speak, they shall render an account for it in the day of judgment. *Matt.* xii. 36.

But He held His peace, and answered nothing. Again the high priest asked Him, and said to Him: Art Thou the Christ, the Son of the blessed God? *Mark* xiv. 61.

Let not thy mouth be accustomed to swearing. *Ecclus.* xxiii. 9.

Let your speech be yea, yea, no, no. *Matt.* v. 37.

Vah! Thou that destroyest the Temple of God. *Matt.* xxvii. 40.

He that blasphemeth, dying let him die. *Lev.* xxiv. 16.

Bless them that curse you. *Luke* vi. 28.

By it we bless God, and by it we curse men. *Jas.* iii. 9.

The prayer of him (the poor) that curseth thee shall be heard. *Ecclus.* iv. 6.

But he began to curse and to swear, saying: I know not this man of whom you speak. *Mark* xiv. 71.

For God is my witness, Whom I serve in my spirit in the Gospel of His Son, that without ceasing I make a commemoration of you; *Rom.* i. 9.

That in the name of Jesus every knee should bow, of those that are in heaven, on earth, and under the earth: *Phil.* ii. 10.

O Lord, how admirable is Thy Name. *Ps.* viii. 1.

My Name is great among the Gentiles. *Mal.* i. 11.

Profane not My Holy Name. *Lev.* xxii. 32.

Let not the naming of God be usual in thy mouth. *Ecclus.* xxiii. 10.

He that despiseth you despiseth Me. *Luke* x. 16.

Behold, before God, I lie not. *Gal.* i. 20.

Thou shalt swear in truth and in judgment and in justice. *Jer.* iv. 2.

Remember Thy servants, to whom Thou sworest. *Ex.* xxxii. 13.

The Lord hath sworn, and He will not repent. *Ps.* cix. 4.

If thou hast vowed anything to God, defer not to pay it. *Eccles.* v. 3.

Whatsoever thou hast vowed, pay it. *Eccles.* v. 3.

The Lord thy God will require it. *Deut.* xxiii. 11.

Love not a false oath . . . which I hate, saith the Lord. *Zach.* viii. 17.

And Jesus said to him: I am. And you shall see the Son of Man sitting on the right hand of the power of God, and coming with the clouds of heaven. *Mark* xiv. 62.

The mother's curse rooteth up the foundation. *Ecclus.* iii. 11.

He loved cursing, and it shall come unto him. *Ps.* cviii. 18.

Solemn Pledge of the Holy Name Society

Blessed be God.

Blessed be His Holy Name.

Blessed be Jesus Christ true God and true Man.

Blessed be the Name of Jesus.

I believe O Jesus

That Thou art the Christ

The Son of the Living God.

I believe all the sacred truths

Which the Holy Catholic Church

Believes and teaches.

I proclaim my love

For the Vicar of Christ on earth.

I promise to give good example,

By the regular practice

Of my faith.

I honor His Divine Name.

I pledge myself against perjury,

Blasphemy, profanity, and obscene speech.

I pledge my loyalty

To the flag of my country

And to the God-given principles

Of freedom, justice, and happiness, for which it stands.

I pledge my support

To all lawful authority both civil and religious.

I dedicate my manhood to the honor of the Sacred Name of Jesus.

And beg that He will keep me faithful to these pledges until death.

Quotations and Resolutions

1. In Nomine Jesu.
2. I am Who am.
3. An oath is an act of Religion.
4. Habit is a poor excuse.
5. Not to keep a good promise is wrong.
6. The Court punishes a perjurer by years of imprisonment; God punishes a perjurer by Eternal Punishment.
7. I will never take the name of God in vain.
8. If I can prevent profane language, I will do so.
9. A curse from a bad habit which one is not trying to overcome is fully responsible.
10. The greater the evil wished, the greater the sin.
11. Do not be hasty and thoughtless in making promises.
12. Taking the pledge is not a vow but a solemn resolution which every honorable person will keep.
13. Cursing is the Language of Hell.
14. Every time I hear a curse word, I will make an act of Reparation to God.

THE THIRD COMMANDMENT

"Remember Thou Keep Holy the Sabbath Day" means more than merely being present at Holy Mass. It is, therefore, none too easy a task for the teacher to imbue the children with the spirit of the liturgy; to make them realize the many blessings that come upon those who keep the Sunday holy; to create for them an atmosphere, so to speak, of a Sunday in accordance with the spirit of the Church and at the same time to satisfy the modern child's natural craving for varied and interesting action.

Spiritual activities, including attendance at Holy Mass, can be and have been made attractive and interesting. We all know what has been done in late years by means of the liturgical movement in promoting an intelligent participation in the services of the Church. The use of the Missal has been especially recommended for this purpose. There is no longer any excuse for children (or grown-ups, for that matter) not being able to follow the priest at Mass, for there are now Missals and other Mass books available at a very reasonable cost:

Benziger Brothers, New York, publishes a translation of *The Child's Daily Missal,* by Dom Gaspar Lefebvre, O.S.B., a complete Missal written for children and containing three hundred illustrations.

There are available several splendid missals for young folks. Especially commendable are *The Dominical Missal* (E. M. Lohmann Company, St. Paul) and *The Small Missal* (The Macmillan Company, New York) which contain the proper of the Mass for all Sundays and the principal feasts, and other useful prayers and devotions.

The Bruce Publishing Company, Milwaukee, Wis., makes a very neat and attractive little book *Mass Prayers,* by Father Garesché, S.J., which has found great favor among high-school students.

Two young priests, the Rev. Paul Bussard, of the St. Paul Cathedral, and Rev. Edward Jennings, of the Basilica of St. Mary, Minneapolis, have recently devised a new plan known as the *Leaflet Missal.* This Missal is a translation of the complete text of the Mass for every Sunday. It is mailed to subscribers for a dollar a year. This means that subscribers will receive 52 booklets, mailed four at a time, throughout the year, each booklet a complete Prayer Book for the specific Sunday, containing all the prayers said by the priest celebrating Mass, and in direct sequence, thus removing all the difficulties that now confuse many persons who try to follow the Mass in the ordinary Missal.

Helps for the Use of the Missal

A Guide for the Roman Missal, sold by the E. M. Lohmann Company, of St. Paul, contains instructions and explanations for the use of the Daily Missal. Many diocesan papers publish weekly a list of Masses for the coming week. This list mentions the feast of the day, the prayers and other texts used at the particular Mass, and the color of the vestment worn by the priest. It is compiled for the convenience of those who use a Missal at Mass. In some schools Missal clubs have been formed. The members of the club meet every Friday for the purpose of discussing different parts of the Mass, the vestments, etc., and for marking their books for the coming week. Incidentally the classroom talks, posters, and projects on the Mass draw new members from week to week.

Other Sunday Devotions

Aside from imposing the obligation of hearing Mass on Sundays, the Church recommends other devotions, such as reception of the sacraments, Benediction, good works, and spiritual reading. In the past, spiritual reading has had little or no attraction for the ordinary child; and a glance at the books that were available will account for the reason. But today religious books for children are made up most attractively and are as interesting as any storybook. Only a few of the many books that are now on the market can be mentioned in connection with this study. There has been no attempt to grade this list according to difficulty, for the reason that many older children may require more simple material to begin with, and also because some of the books written for the lower grades prove just as fascinating to pupils of the higher grades.

The Work of the Teacher

In cultivating a taste for the reading of religious books, just as in other classroom activities, the attitude and enthusiasm of the teacher are the guiding forces. True, a taste for reading, especially for serious reading, cannot be cultivated in a day or a month. But, if the teacher can herself take up one of these books and, with all the delight and abandon of a child read aloud a beautiful selection; if she can become "one of them," reliving with them the stories of the saints and beloved of God, there is no doubt as to the effect upon the children. As has been stated before, spiritual activities of all kinds can be and have been made attractive to children and young people. Notice, for example, the unbounded enthusiasm evidenced in the sodality group organized or reorganized in recent years by Father Daniel Lord, S.J., and his associates. Hear the children tell of the work they are doing for their Mass project, from the collecting of pictures to the making of real vestments for the priest. Learn what they are doing for the missions, the poor, the sick, the ignorant! And why not? They have found a healthful outlet for their youthful enthusiasm and energy, are learning to shoulder responsibility in behalf of their fellow men, are living according to the spirit of the Church, and are at the same time kept away from the harmful influences of unlawful or doubtful pleasures. Does such a program of activities sound dry or unattractive?

Problems for Class Discussion

1. Grandmother is very ill and cannot be left alone. You are asked to remain at home with her while the rest go to Sunday's Mass. May you do so if there is no other Mass? What reason can you give for your answer?

2. Your father takes you on a fishing trip early Sunday morning. You plan on stopping at the next town to hear Mass, but by the time you get there Mass is over. Are you excused?

3. A railroad man has to work on Sundays and cannot hear Mass. May he keep his job? Every few weeks he gets off Sunday mornings just at the time when Mass is half over. He reasons that as long as he could not get a whole Mass there is no need of his going to church. Is he right?

4. A young man is out all Saturday night. Before returning home on Sunday morning he enters church to hear Mass. He sleeps during the greater part of the service. Has he fulfilled his obligation? What must one do in order to fulfill the obligation of hearing Mass on Sundays?

5. A group of boys plan to go camping for three weeks. Fred is sent to select the place and the boys remind him that he must make sure that they will be able to hear Mass on Sundays. Fred returns and says that there is a Catholic church two miles distant. When they arrive, they find that this is not a Catholic church and that there is none near by. Suppose Fred knew all the time that this was not a Catholic church, how much of the blame must he take upon himself? Would it be sufficient for him to confess that he missed a Sunday's Mass? Suppose he really thought he was right, would the matter be different? Should the boys remain at the camp?

6. You are on your way to church on Sunday morning. You meet Lew and ask him to come along. He says he is busy finishing the garage, but that he will make up for the

Mass by going on Monday morning instead. What will you answer? He argues that one Mass is as good as another and further, that the Church has no right to tell him what to do. Answer his arguments.

7. A working girl receives the news that her mother is very ill and she is needed at home. It is Sunday, and in order to be ready for the journey, she will have to do some laundering and sewing. May she do so?

8. Six girls are invited out to a camp for a week-end. They know there is no Catholic church in the vicinity. Several of the girls say that since it is impossible for them to attend Mass they are excused. Are they right?

9. You are on your way to Mass on Sunday. A car ahead of yours is turned over and the driver is injured. If you stop to help him you will miss the only Mass there is at your church. Should you offer your help or go to Mass?

10. Since Mr. Grey owns a radio he does not go to Mass on Sundays. He says he hears Mass and a good sermon every Sunday over the radio and really gets more out of it than when he goes to church. Is he in the right?

11. Jack stays home from Mass on Sunday in order to shovel snow. He says the janitor shovels snow in front of church and if he has a right to do so, so have other people. What will you tell Jack?

12. A farmer and his family were just ready to start for Mass on Sunday morning when they noticed that a heavy storm was threatening. In order to save his crops the farmer went out into the field immediately and also ordered his hired men to do the same. They all missed Mass. Were they justified in doing so? Give reason for your answer.

13. Don wanted to paint the garden fence on Sunday afternoon, but his father would not permit him to do so, as that is servile work and therefore sinful. Don says that their neighbor paints pictures every Sunday and says that it is no sin. Is there any difference?

14. Mary and Jane live on a farm. They have to remain

home from Mass every other Sunday to take care of the children and the house. Mother tells them they ought to recite the Mass prayers at home, but Mary says that will do no good as long as they cannot attend Mass. What do you think about the practice?

15. Mr. Daly goes to a low Mass every Sunday and then goes out fishing or hunting. Mr. Smith, his neighbor, tells him that hearing a Mass is not enough to "keep holy the Sabbath." If you were Mr. Smith, how would you explain the case to Mr. Daly?

16. "You are not keeping the word of God" says a non-Catholic to you. "The Bible says 'Remember thou keep holy the Sabbath Day,' and you Catholics keep Sunday instead." Is there a difference between Sabbath and Sunday? How would you explain the position of Catholics?

17. Mr. Blake is a Catholic, but he does not attend Sunday Mass. He says he will work while he is young and strong and will devote a great deal of time to his soul when he is old and can no longer work. What would you tell him?

18. Marie would not get up immediately when her mother called her on Sunday morning. In consequence she came to Mass after the Offertory. What must she do? Why? Suppose there is no other Mass, what obligation has she?

19. Mr. Payne goes to Mass and other devotions every Sunday. During the week, however, he is engaged in a dishonest business. What do you think of him as a Christian?

20. What does the Consecration of the Mass mean to you? Why do you look at the Host and whisper, "My Lord and my God"?

Biblical References

Thine is the day, and Thine is the night. *Ps.* lxxiii. 16.

God rested on the seventh day from all His work. *Gen.* ii. 2.

The Lord blessed the seventh day and sanctified it. *Exod.* xx. 11.

The Sabbath was made for man. *Mark* ii. 27.

Keep My Sabbath: because it is a sign between Me and you. *Exod.* xxxi. 13.

Therefore hath He commanded thee that thou shouldst observe the Sabbath day. *Deut.* v. 15.

Cursed be he that doth the work of the Lord deceitfully. *Jer.* xlviii. 10.

The seventh day is the Sabbath of the Lord thy God: thou shalt do no work on it. *Exod.* xx. 10.

He that is of God heareth the words of God. *John* viii. 47.

He who soweth sparingly, shall also reap sparingly. *II Cor.* ix. 6.

Six days shalt thou labor, and shalt do all thy works. But on the seventh day is the Sabbath of the Lord thy God; thou shalt do no work on it, thou, nor thy son, nor thy daughter, nor thy manservant, nor thy maidservant, nor thy beast, nor the stranger that is within thy gates. *Exod.* xx. 9, 10.

They grievously violated My Sabbaths. I said therefore that I would pour out My indignation upon them. *Ezech.* xx. 13.

The Apostles plucking ears of corn. *Matt.* xii.

Parable of the sheep falling into the pit on the Sabbath. *Matt.* xii. 11.

Our Lord healed on the Sabbath day. *Matt.* xii. 13. *Luke* xiii. 14.

Stories to Be Looked Up and Told By the Children

The Seventh Day of Creation. The Resurrection. The Descent of the Holy Ghost. Apostles Receiving Power to Forgive Sin. Stories showing the effect of spiritual reading: St. Columbanus, St. Augustine, St. Ignatius Loyola.

Selected Quotations

I have been driven many times to my knees by the overwhelming conviction that I had nowhere else to go; my own wisdom and that of all around me seemed insufficient for the day. — *Abraham Lincoln.*

Nations live only by religion, and it is irreligion which destroys them. — *Msgr. Darboy.*

He who offers God a second place, offers Him *no* place. — *Ruskin.*

If we place our religious progress in outward observance only, our devotion will soon come to an end. — *Imitation,* Bk. I, chap. xi, 4.

The reading, reflection, study, and experience of a long life have strengthened and confirmed my faith in the Catholic Church, which has never. ceased to teach her children how they should live, and how they should die. — *Chief Justice Taney.*

The most perfect act of thanksgiving I know is that in the Gloria, "We give Thee thanks for Thy great glory." — *M. A. Tinckner.*

Two Went Into the Temple to Pray

Two went to pray! Oh, rather say,
One went to brag, the other to pray;

One stands up close and treads on high,
Where the other dares not send his eye.

One nearer to God's altar trod,
The other to the altar's God.
— *Richard Crashaw*

"Some observe the pious custom of reciting the Mass prayers privately, at home, whenever they cannot attend Mass on Sundays or holydays of obligation. This is a very laudable practice as is the habit of reading passages from the Bible or some other good book to make up for the Sunday sermon. This practice is very highly recommended especially to those who habitually cannot attend Sunday Mass. This practice is credited with having saved the faith of many rural families of remote districts, in pioneer days. Persons of isolated districts who follow this practice, keep holy the Lord's day to the best of their ability, when they are not able to attend Mass." — *Rt. Rev. V. Day.*

An Example from Jamaica

It was a warm, sultry Sunday morning in the Island of Jamaica, West Indies. I had left the path that led to the priest's house and had turned my pony into the highway skirting the sea. Five milestones must be passed before I reached my little church.

"Fader," a voice called, "Fader, what time is Communion Mass?"

I stopped the carriage and a Negro boy about eighteen years of age approached. I had seen him at various times in my little church, but he had always disappeared before I could speak to him.

"Are you going to Holy Mass?"

"Yes, Fader. Am I late?"

"Are you walking to Montego Bay?"

"Yes, Fader."

"How far have you walked?"

"From over the mountain, eight miles back."

"You are walking thirteen miles to Holy Mass?"

"Yes, Fader, and I am fasting for Holy Communion."

"Do you intend to walk back home today?"

"Yes, Fader."

I beckoned the boy to ride on the seat beside me. Twenty-six miles on foot and on a hot, tropical road to hear Mass and to receive Holy Communion!

As my pony jogged along to my little church, my thoughts were far away. How many Catholics in the United States would give such a manifestation of love as was shown by this poor Negro boy? What food for meditation this simple, black boy had given to me, a priest of God, on heroic respect and love for the Blessed Sacrament! — *C. J. Mullaly, S.J., in Sacred Heart Almanac.*

The Shameless Beggar

A beggar met a rich man and asked for the price of a meal. The rich man put his hand into his pocket and took out seven silver dollars. Holding them in the palm of his left hand, he divided them into two parts, putting six of the dollars to one side and one to the other. Then he said to the beggar: "Take the six. I want the seventh for myself." The brazen fellow took the six coins offered him, and then, snatching also the remaining dollar, ran away.

"Shame on him!" you say. Yes, but wait a moment; perhaps you have done worse yourself. Of the seven days of the week God gives us six, and demands that we devote the seventh to His service. Every time you neglected Mass on Sunday, you acted like that ungrateful wretch. You not only took the six days given you, but you also refused God the one day He demanded for Himself. Shame on you! How will you feel when you meet your God face to face on judgment day? — *Rt. Rev. V. Day.*

Blessed Thomas More's Respect for Sunday

Blessed Thomas More, Chancellor of England, was an ardent supporter of Catholic belief. For his sincere attachment to it he was at last imprisoned. When going to chapel on Sundays he always appeared very well dressed. One day someone asked him how it was he was so particular in his dress on Sunday, as there were so few to see him in prison; and he at once made answer: "I have always dressed myself with care on Sundays, and on festivals, not to please the world, or through respect for any mortal, but through respect and love for God." — *Life of Blessed Thomas More.*

Result of Irreverence

Pope Pius V had induced a Protestant to enter the Church and was preparing him for baptism. One day the latter was assisting at Mass, but unfortunately the faithful then present were greatly wanting in respect, and the Protestant went away indignant, saying: "No, Catholics do not believe in the Mass: they do not believe in the real presence: if they did, they would behave differently in the presence of God." And he remained a Protestant. — *Cat. en Ex.*

Religious Books Suggested for Reading

Stories of the Saints (for children), published by the International Catholic Truth Society, 407 Bergen Street, Brooklyn, New York, is a series of booklets. The price for each booklet is five cents. Each one deals with a particular saint. The series includes stories of St. Teresa, St. Monica, St. Francis Xavier, St. Sebastian, St. Dorothy, St. Cyril, St. Aloysius, St. Anthony of Padua, St. Elizabeth of Hungary, St. Germaine Cousin, St. Patrick, St. Ignatius Loyola, St. Cecilia, St. Lawrence, St. Francis de Sales, St. Agnes, St. Cyr, St. Frances of Rome, St. George, St. Genevieve, the Forty Martyrs, St. Ignatius of Antioch, St. Benedict, St. Louis, St. Philip, St. Stanislaus, St. Thomas Aquinas, St. Vincent Ferrer, St. Roch, Blessed Thomas More, and St. Vincent de Paul.

Mother Mary Loyola's Books by P. J. Kenedy and Sons, New York, have stories on The King of the Golden City, Jesus of Nazareth, The Child of God, First Communion.

Other books which may be obtained are: The Journeys of Jesus, Sister James Stanislaus, Ginn and Co., Chicago; Our Sacraments, Rev. Wm. R. Kelly, Benziger Brothers, New York; The Little Flower's Love for Her Parents, Sister M. Eleanore, C.S.C., Benziger Brothers, New York; The Little Flower's Love for the Holy Eucharist, Sister M. Eleanore, C.S.C., Benziger Brothers; The Story of St. Francis of Assisi, Sister M. Eleanore, C.S.C., Benziger Brothers; The Lord

Jesus — His Birthday Story, Extension Press, Chicago; Patron Saints for Boys, Mary E. Mannix, Benziger Brothers; Patron Saints for Girls, Mary E. Mannix, Benziger Brothers; Girlhood's Highest Ideal, Rev. Winfred Herbst, S.D.S., Herder, St. Louis; Boyhood's Highest Ideal, Rev. Winfred Herbst, S.D.S., Herder; The Service Beautiful, Rose Graffe, The Mission Press, Techny, Ill.; For Greater Things, Rev. Wm. F. Kane, S.J., Herder, St. Louis; Tell Us Another, Rev. Winfred Herbst, S.D.S., St. Nazianz, Wis.; Catholic Bible Stories, Josephine V. D. Brownson, Extension Press, Chicago, Ill.

Picture Studies[1]

Christ in the Temple, Hoffmann

Sermon on the Mount, Hoffmann

Easter Morning, Hoffmann

Christ Driving Out the Money Changers, Hoffmann

The Last Supper, DaVinci

Pilgrims Going to Church, Boughton

John Alden and Priscilla, Boughton

Chorister Boys, Anderson

Great Cathedrals of the World:

Rheims Cathedral

Cologne Cathedral

Notre Dame Cathedral

Milan Cathedral

Window of Milan Cathedral

St. Peter's, Rome

St. Mark's, Venice

Santa Barbara Mission, California.

Teacher's Outline of the Third Commandment[2]

Principles underlying the Third Commandment:

1. The whole of our time belongs to God.

2. The voice of nature tells us we must devote some time to God.

3. Our only real work here is the salvation of our souls.

4. Man must honor God with his whole being, hence he

---

[1]The above pictures may be obtained from the Perry Pictures Co., Malden, Mass.

[2]According to Howe.

must give Him the service of the body by outward observances.

5. Society also must honor God by fitting worship, hence the public observance of the time given to God.

6. God, by express command, determines the portion of time He requires for Himself.

Sunday:
  I. Not the Sabbath, seventh day of the week, as in the text of *Exodus*.
  II. But Sunday, the first day of the week, called the Lord's Day.
  III. Change made by the Apostles, because on that day:
    1. The work of creation was begun.
    2. Our Lord rose from the tomb.
    3. The Apostles received power to forgive sins.
    4. The Holy Ghost came down on them.
    5. The Jews were no longer the chosen people of the one true God.
    6. The Church was solemnly established.
  IV. The Bible does not teach the observance of Sunday.
  V. Though the particular day was changed, the natural law of observing one in seven remains in force.

Hearing Mass:
  I. The highest form of worship the creature can offer to the Creator.
  II. Hence the Church enjoins attendance at Mass on the Lord's Day.
  III. The whole Mass:
    1. Mortal sin to omit willfully
      a) A notable portion
      b) An essential part
    2. Venial sin to miss a small part without cause.
    3. Willful omission of part of the Mass is

a) Disrespect toward God
b) Distraction to the faithful
c) Perhaps even scandal
IV. Which Mass?
 1. As to obligation, any one Mass, complete in itself.
 2. As to the spirit of the Church, the parish Mass (Council of Trent) with prayers, sermon, etc.
 V. How must we hear Mass?
 1. Bodily presence, so as to see and hear, at least in the action of the people.
 2. Mental presence by attention, etc.
 VI. Obligation of Mass; binding:
 1. Under pain of mortal sin.
 2. All the faithful having the use of reason, unless lawfully excused.
 VII. Reasons excusing from Mass:
 1. Physical impossibility; e.g., sickness, infirmity, weather, etc.
 2. Moral impossibility: e.g., convalescence, serious loss, etc.
 3. Charity.
 4. Prudence is necessary, lest indifference or sloth creep in.
Other means of sanctifying the Sunday:
 1. Hearing instructions.
 2. Afternoon or evening service.
 3. Good works.
Recreation is quite lawful, to refresh body and mind. It should be quiet and moderate.

Resting from Servile Work:
 I. Works divided into three classes:
 1. Liberal, which exercise the mind more than the body: Study, teaching, drawing, etc. Lawful whether done for pay or not.

2. Servile, in which the body is more engaged than the mind: Digging, sewing, etc. Forbidden, whether done for pay or not.
3. Common, done equally by all classes of persons: Traveling, games, etc. Permitted or tolerated, if Mass be heard.
II. Reasons excusing servile work, if Mass be heard, when possible:
   1. Real necessity, which knows no law: To prepare food, to remedy sudden accident, to defend the country in time of war, to avoid some heavy loss.
   2. Charity, which is the end of the law: To attend the sick and infirm, to assist the poor and distressed, without pay in any form.
   3. Piety in the service of God and religion: To adorn the altar or the Church (not build a church).
III. Without these excusing causes, servile works are a desecration of the Sunday.
IV. Guilt of servile works:
   1. Mortal sin
      a) If really laborious
      b) If done for a notable time
   2. Venial sin, if for a short time or for some notable reason.
V. The desecration of Sunday is often punished severely by God, the observance of Sunday visibly rewarded.

Sunday is the Lord's Day and Therefore Eminently Fitted for:
   I. Prayer
      1. The most suitable exercise for this day.
      2. Holy Mass, the best form of prayer.
      3. Afternoon or evening service.
      4. Visits to the Blessed Sacrament.
      5. Private devotions at home.
   II. Sacraments:
      1. Penance to cleanse the soul.

2. Holy Eucharist, the Bread of Life.
3. Spiritual Communion.

III. Instruction:
1. We are bound to know our religion.
2. Willful ignorance of our religion is a sin against Faith.
3. Hence the duty of attending sermons, Sunday school, etc.
4. Responsibility of parents in this regard.
5. How great the ignorance of religion nowadays.

IV. Good Books:
1. Nothing makes such a lasting impression on the soul.
2. No one can go far astray who keeps up spiritual reading.
3. Gather by degrees a few spiritual books for the home library.

Social Advantages of the Third Commandment:
1. Without this day of rest man, engaged in temporal affairs, would soon forget his last end, the sole object of his creation.
2. Without this rest, the bodies of men and animals would wear out before their time.
3. Without this day of prayer and thought, our affections would become a source of calamity: for the passions, guides of those who think only of this life, throw the world into confusion.
4. What must become of the future, with the increasing desecration of the Sunday?
5. In many ways secret societies aim at this, introducing seemingly harmless pleasures. Hence, the need of caution in approving such things harmless in themselves, but calculated to lead from God.

THE FOURTH COMMANDMENT[1]

Honor thy father and thy mother, that
thou mayst be longlived upon the land
which the Lord thy God will give thee.—
Exod. xx. 12.

The above words will be written or printed on the upper part of the blackboard during the time necessary for the study of the Fourth Commandment, as a constant reminder to the children.

BULLETIN

Spiritual	Non-Spiritual

The bulletin board is in charge of the children. They are free to use it, but the pictures and articles supplied

---

[1]Intended for the Fifth Grade.

by them are first to be approved by the teacher. During the study of the commandment, the following pictures will be available:

The Fourth Commandment...............Sinkel
The Selling of Joseph....................Schopin
Joseph's Dream..........................Crespi
Jacob Going to Recover His Son...........Schopin
Prayer of Jacob.........................Doré
Moses Smiting the Rock..................Murillo
Moses Receiving the Tablets..............Raphael
Noah after the Deluge...................Schopin
Infant Samuel ....Reynolds
Jonah ....Doré
Christ-child ....Ittenbach
Flight into Egypt.......................Furst
Miraculous Draft of Fishes...............Raphael
Christ Blessing Little Children...........Plockhorst
Marriage at Cana.......................Tintoretto
Christ Stilling the Tempest...............Doré
Christ Feeding the Multitude.............Murillo
The Little Flower.......................

These pictures are to be pinned on the Spiritual Side, also little poems and quotations of a spiritual nature and dealing with the Fourth Commandment; on the other side of the bulletin any poem, slogan, newspaper clipping, school suggestion, cartoon, not of a spiritual nature, will find place.

In the hands of the children is Deharbe's Catechism and Gilmore's or Schuster's Bible History. Questions 72, 73, 74, 75, 76, 77, 79, 83, 87.

As the teacher, I shall try throughout the day in the various lessons to keep in mind my religion class and when possible refer to the Fourth Commandment; e.g., in spelling I will take such words as obedience, reverence, contempt, superiors.

Instruction Period

I will start with a hymn as usual. The one this week will be "The Fourth Commandment" — Katherine Bainbridge, M. Witmark & Sons, N. Y.

The usual prayer with the intention "for my dear parents."

a) "A long, long time ago, long before Jesus was born, there lived an old Israelite with his twelve sons in a beautiful country home. He loved all his boys with a deep, tender love, but because one of his sons was always so kind and obedient, the father loved him most. So the older boys became jealous and hated their younger brother. The little boy's name was ———."

"All right, Joseph, what was his name?"

"Joseph was his name, Sister."

"Tell us all you know about Joseph."

Finally the story of Joseph with the suggestions of the children is finished by the teacher who throughout has emphasized the obedience, the reverence, and the love which Joseph showed his old father.

The story of Joseph will be evident throughout the instructions on the Fourth Commandment.

b) "Now we have had the story of a little boy's obedience; I think we can find a little girl, too, who was always very good and obedient. Do you know who this is?" (A picture of the Little Flower is shown.)

The teacher will give the story of the Little Flower

74

from any source. (Practical Aids for Catholic Teachers, Sr. Aurelia and Rev. F. M. Kirsch, pages 195–198, gives an interesting account.)

c) "There are just a few minutes left, just enough time to tell you a little story of George Washington. When George was about 16 years old, like so many other boys, he wanted to become a sailor. His dear old mother grieved and was heartbroken, because George was still so young and was going so far away. So the day of his departure arrived, and George said good-by to his old mother and hurried to the ship. But as he was about to board, the sorrow of his dear mother forced him to return. Because of his love and reverence for her, he gave up his cherished desire and the whole course of his life was changed. Do you think that George would ever have become The Father of His Country had he not loved his mother so well?"

"For tomorrow's lesson will you all tell a story on obedience or disobedience? If you want to tell an event in your own lives, you may do so. Perhaps dad or mother can tell you a good story. But remember, children, all the stories must be on the Fourth Commandment. How many will be ready? Oh! that is fine; I'm sure all of your stories will be very good."

Children's Stories Told in Class

The next day's lesson will be the stories of the children told very informally to the class in a socialized recitation. Any questions the children may ask will be open for discussion.

The bulletin board will be in constant use.

Next Recitation

"I have so many, many questions, dear children, about which I want you to tell me. I often wonder what little boys and girls like you would do if certain things that I'm going to ask you about, would happen to you. You know, you and I and everybody must show to parents reverence, love, and obedience, the way Joseph and the Little Flower and George Washington did. Now here are the questions."

Each of the following problems is then presented to them and informally discussed.

Reverence

1. When you were a real little baby, God gave you to mother and dad. They took good care of you; daddy worked hard for you and mother gave you things to eat and watched over you when you were sick. Did you ever thank them for what they did for you when you were very small? Why would it be a very bad thing to speak to them saucily?

2. Did you ever hear a little boy or a little girl call his daddy by a name that was not nice? Maybe he did not call his father that name so he could hear it, but you heard it. What would you do?

3. I know a little girl who will not talk to mother for a long time, even for a whole hour, because mother punished her. What should this girl do to get over her nasty feelings?

4. Sometimes a little boy will talk real meanly about his father because his father will not give him a dime to spend for a movie. What do you think of a boy like that? I wonder if you ever did that? Let's tell Jesus today we will never do that again.

5. It hurts mother and dad very much to scold you. Sometimes children laugh when their parents are scolding them. Why wouldn't you do that?

6. I once saw a little boy run out and slam the door when his father refused to let him stay on the street with the other boys until 9 o'clock. What should that boy do to make up for this act?

7. When you meet your mother on the street, how should you show your respect to her? I think your mother would almost weep if her little boy would run away when he sees her coming, don't you?

8. If daddy ever comes home from work cross because he is so tired, what should his little girl do for him and how should she talk to him?

9. If mother sometimes does things you know are wrong, for instance, suppose she tells you to stay home from school to help with the washing and to tell the teacher you were sick, what would you say to mother about it?

10. If mother dresses in an old-fashioned way, would you be ashamed of her when you are with your friends in a crowd?

11. If a little girl or boy starts scolding about his mother or father, and you hear him, what would you do?

12. Who knows what contempt means? If a child thinks himself so much better and smarter than his parents and acts that way, (contempt) he is sinning against the Fourth Commandment through contempt. Why is that mean?

13. What do you think of your big sister who says to mother: "Oh, shucks! you're an old-timer"?

"Dear children, these are some ways of sinning against reverence due to our parents. Perhaps just these few words will help you to remember what the Catechism teaches us and how we sin against reverence: *despising* our parents, treating them with *contempt*, being ashamed of them.

"Who remembers how Joseph showed reverence to his old father? How did the Little Flower? How did George Washington? And how are you going to do it?"

Answer: By not despising them, not treating them with contempt, not being ashamed of them.

The Next Religion Hour

Meanwhile the bulletin board has had various pictures, suggestions, and poems displayed. Those of the previous days are being arranged in the class booklet called the Fourth Commandment. The children who brought the various articles, original or not, with the help of the teacher will put them into the book and sign them with their names and date of entry.

"Today, children, our lesson will be on the love and obedience we owe to our parents. Yesterday's lesson was on what? (On reverence.) You answered the problems so well yesterday and you showed me how good girls and boys revere their parents. I'm going to give each one of you a very special problem. Think it over for a few moments and then whoever can answer his will read the question for the class and tell the rest what he knows about it. Whoever wants to say some more on the question that has been answered, may do so. While the papers are being distributed, study the words of the Fourth Commandment once more."

The following questions will be typed on small pieces of paper, one on each paper; the questions on love on white paper, and those on obedience on blue, for the purpose of the teacher's convenience in keeping the two sets separate.

Love

1. Why do you love your mother? Your dad?

Answer added to those of the children: Because they hold the place of God, because next to God they are our greatest benefactors.

2. How often do you think a good child would pray for his parents? If you have not prayed for them today you will still do so, won't you?

3. What do you think of a little girl your age who often says, "Mamma, I love you so much," but always gets pouty when her mother says she should wash the dishes or take care of the baby?

4. Must you love your daddy, too, when he is punishing you? What do you think of anyone who would hate his father for punishing him?

5. When mother and father are old and perhaps poor and you are grown up, what will you do for them?

6. If mother is very sad because you are not a good little boy or girl, and is worried because you have not been good at school, or have had a fight with the boys, or have taken some money, what do you think you ought to do to make her happy again?

7. What do you think of your big sister if she tells your mother to go away for the evening because she intends to have *swell* company and is afraid your mother won't be *swell* enough? Will you ever do that?

8. George is a little boy who thinks he knows better than his father. His father says to him: "George, I don't want you to go with Billy Jones any more; he's not the kind of boy I want you to be with." But George knows better and won't take his father's advice and goes with Billy Jones. Do you think George loves his father if he won't listen to him?

9. Mother has made you a new dress but you don't like it; how would you show your love and gratitude to her in spite of your feelings?

10. Mother is sick and very tired. What will you do when you come home from school to show her that you love her?

11. When dad comes home from work so tired, what will you do to show him that you love him?

12. What are some of the jobs you can do at home to show you love your parents?

Obedience

1. Dad says: "Jim, I really wouldn't go swimming today; it's too cold." Now your best friend comes and says: "Jim, swimmin's fine; come on." What would you do?

2. Mother has told you to come home right after school. But your little friend tells you to come with her because she is home alone and that she is going to make some fudge. What would an obedient girl do? What excuse could a disobedient girl make later to her mother? What would you think of her?

3. Dad said: "You stay home tonight. No movies." Dad and mother go away for the evening and you know it. Charlie Chaplin is on just around the corner and you can get back long before your parents come home and they will never know anything about it. Will you go to that movie? What do you think of one who would go after his father has said this?

4. Mother wants you to eat spinach and to drink milk. You don't like it and begin to grumble and get stubborn at the table. You know that is wrong, but you always do it. How can you get over that habit?

5. Mother has told her little girl to watch the baby on the lawn. The fire engine comes by and she runs along, forgetting all about the baby. After an hour she comes back. A little voice had whispered to her after

a little while that she is disobedient, but she would not listen. Baby is still safe on the lawn. Should the girl tell mother what she had done or should she say nothing about it because the baby's all right? What would you do?

6. Sunday afternoon there are services at church. Dad says: "Son, you go to church this afternoon, and then you may go to the park." You run off to church, kneel about two minutes in the back, then run out to the park. Were you obedient?

7. Mother calls at 7:00 a.m. "Ed, time to get up." "Yep." But you don't do it. 7:15 — "Ed, get up!" — Mother again. 7:30 — "Ed, I'll get dad if you don't get up this minute!" And up you are. What kind of boy will this sort of action make you?

8. Father says: "You mow the lawn this morning." You obey but you are grumbling and grouching the whole morning. How are you sinning against the Fourth Commandment?

9. An act of obedience is very hard. You obey just because father has said so. Couldn't you find a better reason for obeying? Perhaps you could find more than one; try to.

10. Some little boys and girls will run away when they know they are going to be punished for disobeying. What kind of boys and girls will they grow up to be?

11. Do you see any rewards God has promised in the Fourth Commandment to children who obey? What are they?

12. What punishments has God prepared for those children who are disobedient to their parents in very important cases? Can you tell the class how a big man might commit a mortal sin against his parents?

13. What punishments has God prepared for those children who are disobedient to their parents in small matters?

14. How long must a boy or girl obey parents?

15. If a little boy of your age usually is disobedient, how can he learn to become obedient?

Next Recitation in Religion

"Children, your Catechism tells you that you sin against obedience in three ways: By refusing to obey; by not taking your parents' advice; and by not accepting the punishment. Try to remember them."

"You have answered so many questions on the reverence, love, and obedience you must show your parents. Must you show these to any other people? That's fine, George; Yes, to the School, to the Church. Now there is one more group." — "Tell me, Ed, why didn't you shoot big fire crackers last Fourth of July?" — "Who can give me a better reason than just because you couldn't buy any?" — "That's true. But why do you have to obey the laws?" — "Not only because you will be arrested, but especially because God commands you to obey all lawful superiors, and that is what the government is. Today we will have our last set of problems, how and why we must obey School, Church, and Country. We shall start with School first. Who can tell me how children can be disobedient in school?"

After the children have given their own, the following points will be taken, omitting those the children themselves have suggested.

School

1. The teacher has left the room and you know you should be doing quiet work. You know, too, you can get most of the boys and girls to talk if you want to. Would you be more disobedient than a boy who would just whisper to his neighbor, if you were to start talking?

2. You don't like your teacher sometimes because you think she is cross. You try to tease her by being naughty and when she calls on you, you get saucy. Why must you obey even a teacher whom you do not like?

3. A little girl is stubborn because she thinks she did not deserve to be scolded. Even if she didn't deserve it, what else might she do to show the teacher that she is innocent instead of becoming stubborn?

4. If you have said something that is very disrespectful about your teacher and which would lower her in the minds of the other children, making them act naughtily, what would you have to do to make up for this?

5. Your teacher is sad today because you and some other little children were naughty in school or at recess; wouldn't you care or what would you do about it?

6. You see your best friend go to another boy's locker and you know the school forbids this. Soon the boy discovers that his ball is gone. What would you do about it?

7. You may not take books home from a shelf. You started a story and want to finish it, so you slip the book between your other ones and go off with it, intending to return it in the morning.

8. If the teacher tells the class to close their books but one little boy in the back does not obey except when the teacher is looking in his direction, what would you say to that boy to show him he is doing himself much harm?

9. How do you like this resolution: I am going to obey the rules of the school to keep out of trouble?

10. Did you ever think that the way you obey and act in school is most likely the way you do it at home?

Church

1. Dad has given you five cents to put into the collection box. On the way you buy four cents' worth of candy and put one cent into the box. Besides deceiving, how would you be failing in your duty toward the Church?

2. You know you should not talk in church when the Blessed Sacrament is there, but your friend next to you starts talking; what will you do about it?

3. Some little boy says very bad things about the priest which he has heard his father say. He is saying this to a crowd of boys and you also hear him. Have

you any duty to stop him and how would you do it?

4. You know you must go to Mass on Sunday. Your father is not a Catholic, and your mother is gone. Dad tells you Saturday night that he and you will leave for the lake at 5 o'clock. You have not had the chance to go to Mass. What will you do or say? Are you obliged to object?

5. The Church law commands you to hear Mass on Sunday. People often come to Mass after the Offertory and leave before Mass is over. Do they sin against obedience or because they have not heard Mass? Especially do newsboys do that. What do you say about it?

State

1. To be a good citizen a little boy or girl must obey the traffic rules; besides running the risk of being hurt, aren't children disobeying at such times if they run their own way as they please? Is that a sin?

2. You must help keep the streets clean. After school you have banana peelings, paper bags, etc., which you throw into a back street when nobody sees you. What kind of boy might such continued action make you?

3. You have chicken-pox but you play with the neighbor children anyway when their mother and your mother don't see you. Are you disobeying a law?

4. Why should you not go fishing for bass in the early spring? If you happen to catch a nice big bass, what will you do with it?

5. Why should you obey the laws even if you don't like them?

"Now, children, can you answer this question: Who, besides our parents, are those to whom we owe reverence, love, and obedience?"

Answer: Our teachers, our spiritual and temporal superiors in school, in church, in the state.

* * *

"Let us try for our tomorrow's lesson to tell as many Bible History stories as we can find which in some way refer to the Fourth Commandment. Each one of you may select the story you like best and during your silent-reading period this afternoon may use your Bible History to prepare. As soon as you have your story selected, if I am not at a recitation, bring it to me so that not too many will take the same story."

The teacher will have the following list ready for suggestions:

Adam and Eve	Absalom
Fall of the Angels	Birth of St. John the Baptist
Building of the Ark	Flight into Egypt
Noe's offering at his return	Jesus at 12 years of age
Isaac	The wedding at Cana
Joseph	Joseph and Mary go to
Moses in the bulrushes	Bethlehem
Moses and the Red Sea	Multiplication of the loaves
Jonas	Jesus Blesses the Children
Solomon and his mother	Draft of Fishes
Tobias	Jesus and Mary
Samuel	

These stories will last at least for two recitations. As the story involves a certain phase of the Fourth

Commandment, the teacher will review the corresponding Catechism question.

Drill and Summary

The next recitation will have for its aim the final drill of the Catechism questions. If the catechist does not demand verbatim work, just a final talking over of all the questions in the recitation period will be sufficient. An objective test will serve as a basis for further drill and also for the two-weeks' grade.

The story of Joseph has been woven in throughout the work of the past weeks and so will be ready for an informal dramatization for which the children shall choose the cast. No child will be forced to take part. The scenes will be very simple, the children not at all held to any memorized words, but merely to a proper sequence of events. The children have been informed of this dramatization in the early part of the week and any original ideas in dress, in setting, may be resorted to. No doubt an invitation offered to the catechist and to Sister Superior will increase the interest and enthusiasm.

The booklet, the Fourth Commandment, worked out by the children, will be placed where it may be accessible to one and all.

Bulletin Board
Little deeds of kindness, little words of love,
Make of earth an Eden like the heaven above.
— *F. S. Osgood*

No matter what you do
  At home or at your school,
Always do your best,
  There is no better rule.
              — *Phoebe Cary*

If a task is once begun
Never leave it till it's done;
Be the labor great or small
Do it well or not at all.
              — *Phoebe Cary*

My blessed task from day to day
Is nobly, gladly to obey.
              — *Harriet Kimball*

For mother-love and father-care
For brothers strong and sisters fair,
For love at home and here each day,
Father in heaven we thank Thee.

  Be kind and be gentle
    To those who are old,
  For kindness is dearer
    And better than gold.

Good little boys should never say,
  "I will" and "Give me these,"
O no! that never is the way;
  But "Mother, if you please."

  I know who is hiding
    In the wee white Host,
  Jesus there is biding,
    He whom I love most.
              — *Faber*

He that striketh his father or mother shall be put to death. He that curseth his father or mother shall die the death.— *Exod.* xxi. 17.

With all thy soul, fear the Lord and reverence His priests.— *Ecclus.* vii. 31.

Honor the person of the aged man.—*Lev.* xix. 32.

Father and Mother are your Best Friends.

Be a Pal to father and father will be a Pal to you.

My mother is the BEST MOTHER in the world.

Objective Tests

Best Answer:

Check the answer of the one you think is best.

1. I must obey my parents
   - *a*) Because they will reward me if I do.
   - *b*) Because they will punish me if I don't.
   - *c*) Because they take the place of God.
2. I love my parents because
   - *a*) They work for me.
   - *b*) The Fourth Commandment obliges me to.
   - *c*) Because they love me.
3. I honor my parents because
   - *a*) They are very smart.
   - *b*) They are so good.
   - *c*) If I do not, God will punish me.
4. I must obey my teachers because
   - *a*) I love them.
   - *b*) I want some good marks.
   - *c*) They take my mother's place.
5. I must obey the rules of the city because
   - *a*) I am a citizen.
   - *b*) If I do not, the policeman will get me.
   - *c*) I want to be a good Catholic.

True-False

Write the word true or false in the lines at the end of each statement, which will make the statement correct:

1. Every sin against the Fourth Commandment is a venial sin. ―――――

2. Joseph is a type of Christ. ―――――

3. Parents may do with their children what they want. ―――――

4. All the brothers of Joseph hated him. ―――――

5. Joseph did not love his brothers; that is why he told on them. ―――――

6. Jacob went to Egypt because Joseph was the ruler of Egypt. ―――――

7. I must obey my parents in all things. ―――――

8. Dad usually knows better than I. ―――――

9. The Fourth Commandment is the only one with a promise. ―――――

10. If I am living with my parents when I am 21 years old, I am still bound by the Fourth Commandment. ―――――

Fill in the blanks with the correct words:

1. We sin against the Fourth Commandment by not showing ―――――――, and ――――――― to our parents.

2. The greatest model for girls and boys in obedience is ―――――――.

3. The next greatest model in obedience is ―――――.

Name ten Bible History stories or persons which relate to the Fourth Commandment.

Special Biblical References

Obedience: Jesus; and He was subject to them. — *Luke* ii. 51.

Love: "Hear my son, the words of my mouth and lay them as a foundation in thy heart." — *Tob.* iv. 2.

Joseph and his old father.

Honor: Solomon and his mother. — *III Kings* xi. 19.

Reward: Isaac allowed himself to become a victim; in reward the promise given Abraham passed over to him and the Messias sprang from his seed. — *Gen.* xxii.

Tobias: the protection of the Archangel Raphael and the great temporal prosperity. — *Tob.* v. 1.

Children rewarded: Abel, Isaac, Joseph, Samuel.

Punishments: Absolom for rebelling against his father has his hair caught on an oak tree and while so hanging is pierced by his enemy with a lance. — *II Kings* xviii. 18.

Children punished: Cain, Sons of Heli, Absolom, Cham.

Ecclesiastical Authority: Honor God with all thy soul and give honor to the priests. — *Ecclus.* vii. 33.

Civic Authority: Let every soul be subject to higher powers: for there is no power except from God. — *Rom.* viii. 1.

Give unto Cæsar the things that are Cæsar's, unto God the things that are God's. — *Matt.* xxii. 21.

THE FIFTH COMMANDMENT

This study of the Fifth Commandment, planned for the intermediate grades, again follows the outlines of the Fourth and of the Second Commandments.

Suggestions for the Bulletin Board

Again the bulletin boards, the blackboards, or the burlap borders should be in constant use. The children will take much interest and pride in securing suitable material. As in the preceding studies, the following are suggested for the boards:

1. Quotation Booklets or Cards
2. Pictures illustrative of Kindness, Love of Neighbor, Forgiveness, Charity, etc.
3. Art Pictures
4. Little Poems
5. Slogans (Original ones on the part of the pupils create friendly rivalry)
6. Posters
7. Resolutions suggested by the children
8. Books, Magazines, Illustrated Stories (Table Exhibit)

Editor's Note. Sister Catherine stresses the importance of training for kindness in teaching the Fifth Commandment. Her outline is well adapted for immediate use in the classroom. The *Catholic School Journal* would be interested in the result obtained from this procedure.

Recitation Periods

As a general rule, the more freely the children express themselves in these *socialized recitations* and in the *discussion groups,* the better. It is especially through these unconscious revelations that the alert teacher can study the characters of her children, and thus make those little but important contacts with them individually which carry their influence all through life. The situations, offered a little later in this work, are again mere suggestions. Each teacher will meet many different situations in her group, upon which she ought to dwell, as she sees them to be the more profitable for her children.

After the many stories and situations have been discussed in class, the children will incidentally have learned the contents of the questions of the Catechism. The drill upon these questions will follow and will, in most cases, entail comparatively little work.

Correlation with Other Subjects

Throughout the day the teacher can refer naturally to any phase of the Fifth Commandment. In the English class, in the silent-reading period, literary works, such as are suggested in the study, can be used. Also words occurring in the Catechism on the Fifth Commandment can be taken as the spelling lesson. Even in the arithmetic class, problems involving the giving of money for charitable institutions, the budget necessary for a society, as that of The Infant Jesus Society, the child's own problem of how much or what percentage of his spending money he will put into the regular-Sunday collection, will influence his attitude toward unselfishness.

The prevailing spirit of the weeks spent in the study of this commandment must necessarily be that of Love of Neighbor, Charity, Unselfishness, Meekness — the Spirit of the Gentle Savior.

Introductory Lesson

About two weeks preceding the study of the Fifth Commandment, in the English classes, the children may begin to write a little play of two or three scenes based upon the Parable of the Good Samaritan. The teacher will offer her suggestions, but again as much as possible she should let the children be free to do their own task. The children will then select the characters, who will present the little drama in the introductory period. Simple costumes can readily be improvised. The teacher will gladly offer her services, thus insuring success. A dramatization of Blessed Herman Joseph and the Infant Jesus, instead of that of the Good Samaritan, could be given. *Practical Aids for Catholic Teachers,* by Father Kirsch and Sister Aurelia, pages 244 and 245, gives a dramatization of it. Should a general assembly take place, the class might present the play for the school. With the permission of the Sister Superior or the principal, a penny admittance fee for the smaller children and a nickel for the older ones, will prove interesting. The money so obtained could be placed in the mite box or into the poor box.

The Following Recitations

These stories and situations may be helpful:

Old-Testament Stories

Cain and Abel
Noah and the Ark (Preservation and use of animals)
Joseph in prison
Joseph repays his brethren with love
The patience of Job
The giving of the Ten Commandments

Abraham's love of peace and hospitality
Joseph and his brethren
Murmurs of the Jews and their punishment
Ruth
Jonathan's love for David
Saul's hatred and his punishment

New-Testament Stories

Mary visits Elizabeth
The Nativity, how God loves man
The Shepherds and the Wise Men
The Marriage at Cana
The Paralytic
The Eight Beatitudes
The Spiritual and Corporal Works of Mercy
The Ten Lepers
Miracle of the Loaves and Fishes

Jesus, the Friend of Children (Scandal)
The Unforgiving Servant
The Good Samaritan
The Lord's Prayer
The Good Shepherd
The Prodigal Son (Mercy of the Father)
The Rich Man and Lazarus
Judas
The Crucifixion (The supreme act of Love and Forgiveness of Enemies)

Stories of the Saints of God

The Blessed Virgin, Mother of Mercy
St. Elizabeth of Hungary
St. Bernard
St. Nicholas

St. Francis and the Wolf of Gubbio
St. Anthony of Padua
St. Theresa
St. Vincent de Paul

St. Frances de Chantal
St. Francis de Sales
St. Bernadine of Sienna
St. Peter Nolasco
St. Camillus

St. Francis Xavier
St. Raymond
St. Stephen (Forgiveness)
St. Arsenius and the pillow
(Scandal and Restitution)

Various Stories

Father Damian and the lepers
Stories of Priests and Sisters in their attendance upon the sick and dying; teachers in schools
Activities of the St. Vincent de Paul Society

The Red Cross
The Holy Childhood Society
Magazine stories from the Little Missionary, the Sacred Heart Messenger, the Sunday Visitor

Art Pictures*

The following pictures should be at hand:

The Christ-Child — Ittenbach
The Selling of Joseph—Schopin
The Marriage at Cana — Tintoretto
Christ Feeding the Multitude — Murillo
Charity — Thayer

Christ Healing the Blind—Bida
Lazarus at the Rich Man's Gate — Doré
The Beggar Boys — Murillo
A Helping Hand — Renouf
Christ in the Home of Peasants — L'Hermite

Daily Situations

1. What do you think is the chief reason we may not kill our neighbors or ourselves?

2. Our body is like a rented house. The owner of the house can do what he wants to with it, but the renter may not. How does a renter treat the house? How, then, should we treat our body?

3. A robber comes into the house. Your father must shoot or be shot himself. Should he try just to wound the robber or to kill him? Why?

*These pictures may be obtained from the Perry Picture Co., Malden, Mass.

97

4. Some children are too lazy to study. How do they fail against the Fifth Commandment?

5. Many little boys and girls come to school with dirty hands, face, and clothes. Are they committing faults, perhaps even venial sins, against the Commandment? (Spreading diseases, etc.)

6. So many children in this class are always regular, punctual, and industrious. What kind of men and women do you expect them to become?

7. Many of you have seen a drunken man on the street. What do you think of such a man? Would you like to be a man like that? If not, what must you start doing today already? (Mortification in small things.)

8. Why is it such an evil for a man or woman to become intoxicated? (Brings them to the level of beasts, lose their reason.)

9. How many evil results can you mention because of drunkenness in a family?

10. How many good results can you mention because there is no drunkenness in the family?

11. Who can tell how hard physical work, especially in the fresh air, can save health? (Peace of mind, better circulation, appetite.)

12. Some children think it is "smart" to hang on cars, to run in front of coming automobiles or trains. Are these acts sinful? (They expose themselves unnecessarily to fatal accidents.)

13. A friend has told you that swimming is fine.

Your father said the water is still too cold. The boy calls you a coward because you tell him the water is too cold. What will you do about it?

14. A friend tells you in the presence of a group of younger children, that one of your classmates has cheated in an examination, has stolen something, has lied. He is not absolutely sure, but he tells it anyway. How can you prevent the sin of scandal with these younger children?

15. If you told others the same stories about this boy, and they in turn told others, what do you think of the guilt in your case?

16. Even if you know these things to be true about him, why should you refrain from telling your friends about them? Whom should you tell?

17. You have been invited to go apple-stealing. You know the boys will call you a coward if you do not join them. Tell the class what you would say to these boys.

18. Another boy has induced you to do something wrong. You have induced someone else; and he, another, and so on. This is a real sin of scandal. How can you gain absolution from your sin and how must you confess it?

19. At times little girls are very jealous of one another. When some child has received a reward, how can you overcome your feeling of envy or jealousy? Often say, "Jesus, help me to become a noble child."

20. I have often heard children say: "I just hate

John. I can't stand him." If these children hate the evil qualities of John, does that prove that they hate John himself? In what does the sin consist?

21. What do you think a good way of treating a child who always picks a quarrel on the playground or in the games?

22. Do you think it is a joke to trip anybody purposely? Mention some of the results to such a thoughtless act.

23. When you cause suffering through such a foolish joke, are you obliged to pay the bills due to doctors, hospitals, etc.?

24. Sometimes groups of boys or girls talk indecently. You don't want that to continue. How will you try to stop it?

25. If by your misconduct in church or in school, you are the cause that others act in the same way, how must you confess it?

26. It seems true that children who are cruel to animals grow up into hard-hearted, evil men and women. What should you do if you ever see a child cruel to any animal or insect?

27. If you have vexed your parents or your schoolmates, what will you do to make up for this?

28. What do you think of a boy who is always calling others names, but who gets very angry as soon as he thinks he is offended?

29. How can you develop a calm, even temper? What do you think of a boy or a girl who becomes angry very easily?

30. Some good resolutions ought to be made during our study of the Fifth Commandment. Each one of you think of the one you are going to make in order to become more pleasing to God.

Literary Selections

As suggested above, these selections may be used during the English periods and during silent reading:

Bible Stories (The masterpiece in literature)

Uncle Frank's Mary, by Clementia

Children of the Log Cabin, by Delamare

Legends of the Holy Child, by Lutz

Patron Saints for Boys, by Mannix

Patron Saints for Girls, by Mannix

Story of Columbus, by Pratt

Little Heroine of Poverty Flat, by Comfort

Fairy of the Snows, by Finn

The Bird's Christmas Carol, by Wiggins

Mrs. Wiggs of the Cabbage Patch, by Alice H. Rice

Abridged Christmas Carol, from Dickens

King of the Golden River, by Ruskin

'Lisbeth, by Waggaman

The Selfish Giant, by Wilde

St. Francis, by Williams

Poems Worth Knowing, (Grade V), by Faxon

The Vision of Sir Launfal, by Lowell

Snowbound, by Whittier

Poems Every Child Should Know, by Burt

Books of Famous Verse, by Repplier

Suggested Poems for the Bulletin Boards

Kind words are like sunbeams
That sparkle as they fall;
And loving smiles are sunbeams,
A light and joy to all.

—

In the world is darkness,
So we must shine —
You in your small corner,
And I in mine.

— *Emily Miller*

101

The world is so full of a number of things,
I'm sure we should all be as happy as kings.
— *Stevenson*

—

Do not look for wrong or evil,
    You will find them if you do;
As you measure for your neighbor,
    He will measure back to you.
— *Alice Cary*

—

Cross words are like ugly weeds;
    Pleasant words are like fair flowers;
Let us sow sweet thoughts for seeds,
    In these garden-hearts of ours.

—

Every gentle word you say,
One dark spirit drives away;
Every gentle deed you do,
One bright spirit brings to you.
— *Virginia Harrison*

—

Kind hearts are the gardens,
    Kind thoughts are the roots,
Kind words are the flowers,
    Kind deeds are the fruits.

Take care of your garden,
    And keep out the weeds;
Fill, fill it with sunshine,
    Kind words and kind deeds.
— *Alice Cary*

—

Just being happy
    Is a fine thing to do;
Looking on the bright side,
    Rather than the blue.

—

A cheerful spirit gets on quick;
A grumbler in the mud will stick.

God make my life a little staff,
Whereon the weak may rest;
That so what health and strength I have
May serve my neighbors best.

—

God make my life a little light,
Within the world to glow;
A tiny flame that burneth bright
Wherever I may go.

God make my life a little flower,
That giveth joy to all,
Content to bloom in native bower,
Although its place be small.

God make my life a little song,
That comforteth the sad;
That helpeth others to be strong,
And makes the singer glad.
— *Matilda Edwards*

Hurt no living thing;
Ladybird nor butterfly,
Nor moth with dusty wings,
Nor cricket chirping cheerfully,
Nor grasshopper so light of leap
Nor dancing gnat, nor beetle fat,
Nor harmless worms that creep.
— *Christina Rosetti*

—

Speak gently, kindly, to the poor,
Let no harsh tone be heard;
They have enough they must endure
Without an unkind word.

—

Good breeding is the result of much good sense, some good nature, and a little self-denial for the sake of others.—*Chesterfield.*

—

Popularity is not due to great things or special charms, but to little kindnesses that anyone could do, but most people overlook; and saying pleasant things that anyone might say, but only few take the trouble to do so.

—

Persons should direct, not obey their appetites.

—

It is almost a definition of a gentleman to say that he is one who never inflicts pain. — *Cardinal Newman.*

—

If Wisdom's ways you wisely seek,
　Five things observe with care:
Of whom you speak, to whom you speak,
　And how, and when, and where.

—

Be courteous to all.
Speak evil of none.
Hear before judging.

—

Think before speaking.
Hold your tongue.
Be kind to the distressed.
Ask pardon of all wrongs.
Be patient towards everybody.
Disbelieve most ill reports.
Honesty is the best policy.
　　　　　—Franklin

—

Do unto others as you would have them do unto you.

—

Let me be kind in word and deed,
Just for today.

THE SIXTH AND NINTH COM-MANDMENTS

It is evident that the Sixth and Ninth Commandments do not lend themselves to intimate group discussion as readily as do other Commandments, especially where boys and girls are grouped together. Stress has therefore been laid more on the virtue of purity than on the opposite vice. Nevertheless, the obligation to instruct the children carefully and properly in these Commandments remains, or becomes, if anything, more serious.

Those who have come into close contact with adolescents and have interested themselves in their spiritual and temporal welfare outside of the classroom, must realize how necessary it is to give careful guidance and instructions, especially in connection with problems of purity. True, we feel rightfully that the home should take care of such matters, at least to some extent. But in the first place, many parents admit frankly that they do not know how to go about it. In the second place, there remains a number of children who, because of unfortunate circumstances, cannot or do not go to their parents for information; and lastly, there are only too many boys and girls who get their information anywhere else but in the home. And what information! Can we wonder that their outlook on life is anything but beautiful? It may be mentioned that young people have often stated that if they had received proper instruction at the right time and in the right place, they would have been spared much worry and uneasiness.

In the meantime, what is to be done? Teachers can, first of all, impress upon the parents their obligations to the children in this regard, and recommend, or better still, offer to them helpful books which render the task comparatively simple and easy.

The father is the logical person to instruct a boy in these matters, and for girls, the mother is the natural teacher. If the father or the mother is incompetent in this regard, the other parent may instruct both the boys and girls.

Instruction by the Teacher

For a teacher of the elementary grades, about the most that can be done is to give some *general* instructions on purity and its opposing vice. The Church is of the opinion that detailed instruction on this matter, when given to a group, does more harm than good.

It is entirely possible that the teacher will be asked privately by individual pupils, regarding the processes of generation. In such cases the pupil should be earnestly and kindly referred to his parents or to his father confessor, and only when these two sources fail is the teacher justified in giving such instructions.

One warning may not be out of place. It is one thing to answer a question by simply saying, "No, that may never be done!" It is quite another to develop the right attitude toward certain laws and regulations by showing their reasonableness. It is the duty of the parents, the confessor, or the one who gives this instruction to develop such attitudes.

Correlation With Other Work

While discussing one of the problems here presented — that of pictures in one's private room — a group of girls worked out a plan for furnishing an "ideal" room for a young girl. Out of this plan has developed the study of worth-while art pictures, their place in the home, their history, the artist, etc. Other problems would, no doubt, suggest similar projects. The study of Alice Meynell's poem "The Shepherdess" for the girls, and of Alfred Tennyson's "Sir Galahad" for the boys, a Mary Book with pictures and poems referring to Mary's purity — these are but a few of the suggestions that come to mind.

Problems for Discussion

1. There are three Saints always pictured with a lily. Do you know who they are? Why do they carry a lily? Of what is the lily a symbol?

2. What is meant by the proverb: Birds of a feather flock together. Do you believe the saying always true? James goes with bad companions, but he says the boys can't harm him; in fact, he is doing his best to make them better. Do you think he will succeed? What comparison could you make to prove your point to James?

3. You and your little sister are out in the country for a walk. Your sister is very thirsty and wants to take a drink

from the river. Would you allow her to do that? Why not? Would that be worse than to take her to a show that is not good? Or to hear a wicked story, or read a bad book? What difference is there? Do you know of a scripture text that would apply here?

4. Ben takes you to his home for the first time and shows you his room. The walls are filled with indecent pictures. Could you judge from them what kind of companion Ben is? Would the pictures be a sure sign that he is bad or could there be another reason for his having them? What should you do in either case?

5. Ann and her sister go to a party. They soon learn that the people at the party are not behaving decently. Ann wants to go home, but her sister says they would offend their friends by leaving now, and furthermore they would be laughed at. What would you do under the circumstances?

6. Jack was sitting by the window and reading. All of a sudden he caught himself in the act of daydreaming and realized that his thoughts had drifted to forbidden things. Had Jack committed a sin up to this time? What should he do now? He takes up his book and begins to read again, but finds that he cannot get rid of his evil thoughts. Can you suggest other remedies?

7. Frank is a lazy boy who spends most of his time in idle dreaming or lying around doing nothing. Joseph, his brother, is always occupied with something. He is always reading, or working, or playing. Which of the two boys has the better chance of remaining morally good? Why? Can you find a proverb that will answer this question?

8. Dorothy is not careful about dressing modestly. Her mother tells her she is doing wrong, but Dorothy answers that she is only doing what other girls are doing and that it has not harmed her yet, nor will it harm her. Do you agree? Do you know that the Sunday Visitor is carrying on a Crusade for Modesty in dress? Look it up and see whether you would not like to join.

9. Grace's older sister wants her to go along to a dance. Grace knows that the place has a very bad reputation, but her sister says that they will stay with their own group and that, after all, it's up to a girl to keep her place. Do you think Grace should go?

10. If your parents or your pastor warned you that the water you were about to drink is poisoned, would you drink the water anyway, just because you could see nothing wrong with it? Do you think people who want to poison others through bad reading would be foolish enough to label the books "Poison"? Do they want you to see that they are bad? Then do you think it wise not to listen to the warnings of your parents or your pastor in regard to dangerous amusements, such as dances, movies, etc.?

11. If a person has taken poison by mistake, can something be done to help him, if it is discovered in time? Do you think is is as easy to discover the poisoning of the mind and heart and to apply a remedy? Which poison works more slowly and secretly?

12. A certain man has some rare lily plants which he wishes to raise in his garden. If he wants to make sure that these lilies develop to their fullest, what will he have to do? A child's innocence is a thousand times more precious than the most beautiful flower. What, then, must a child do, to protect its innocence?

13. Suppose that the man who owned the beautiful lilies showed them to some friends, do you think he would allow them to handle their lovely white chalices? Why not? Does not the man himself handle the flowers? Does it make any difference who handles them? If, when the man wasn't looking, people touched and fondled the flowers, what would happen to them? Would they still be an ornament to the garden? If not, what would probably be done with them? Often young girls and boys want to touch and pet one another. The result is very much like it would be with the lilies, only much sadder. Young girls especially, must have

about them a certain reserve which says to everybody that has no right to touch them, "Keep off!" Only in that way they can protect themselves from the danger of having their purity soiled and tarnished, if not altogether lost. A manly boy will respect every girl and never attempt to put his hands on her. He will feel it his duty to protect a girl who is either too timid to defend herself or has not enough sense to know better.

14. Why did God choose Mary as His mother and St. Joseph as His foster-father? Why was He particularly fond of St. John and of little children? Do you know what special favor virgins will enjoy in heaven? Who were the Vestal Virgins, and what favors did they enjoy?

15. When the angel Gabriel announced to Mary, the purest of all creatures, that she was to become the Mother of God, she was puzzled. However, she did not hesitate to ask the angel how that could be possible. When you are puzzled about things you hear or discover, and which you feel should not be talked about openly, where should you go for information? Would it be right to go to companions in place of the confessor or parents? Remember, that whatever God has made is in itself good and was created for a good purpose. It is only when God's gifts are misused that the actions become sinful. Therefore, when a doctor or a nurse handles the human body, or when is it handled for the sake of cleanliness, there is no wrong in it. But when it is done without reason or for the sake of pleasure, then it is very wrong and sinful and often brings on sickness and an early death.

16. Do you know of any great sinners who have become saints? The following act of consecration to the Blessed Virgin has been highly recommended by priests to those who wish to free themselves from sins against the Sixth Commandment or to protect themselves against such sins. Say it every day with all your heart, especially when you find yourself in danger.

Prayer to the Blessed Virgin, especially recommended to those who desire the gift of purity:

My Queen! my Mother! I give myself entirely to thee; and to show my devotion to thee, I consecrate to thee this day my eyes, my ears, my mouth, my heart, my whole being, without reserve. Wherefore, good Mother, as I am thine own, keep me, guard me, as thy property and possession. (100 days' indulgence, if once a day in the morning and evening a Hail Mary is said with this prayer. Pius IX, Aug. 5, 1851.) [Racc. 288.]

Ejaculations

My Queen! my Mother! remember I am thine own. Keep me, guard me, as thy property and possession. — Hail Mary, etc. (40 days' indulgence, each time. Pius IX, Aug. 5, 1851.)

To thee, O Virgin Mother, never touched by stain of sin, actual or venial, I commend and confide the purity of my heart. (100 days' indulgence, once a day. Pius IX, Nov. 26, 1854.)

O Mary conceived without sin, pray for us who have recourse to thee.

Stories for Reference

Bible Stories:

The Deluge. *Gen.* vii.	Sodom and Gomorrha. *Gen.*
The Destruction of Sichem.	xix. 24.
Gen. xiv.	Egyptian Joseph
Noe's Sons	

Stories of Saints: (Many others can be supplied by the children)

St. Joseph	St. Agnes
St. Anthony	St. Rose of Lima
St. Aloysius	The Little Flower
St. Stanislaus Kostka	St. Dorothy
St. Casimir	St. Lucy
St. John Berchmans	St. Cecilia

Other References:

King of the Golden City. — *Mother Mary Loyola*
The Story of Sir Galahad and the Holy Grail
The Vestal Virgins

*Poems for Study:**

The Shepherdess — *Alice Meynell*
Sir Galahad — *Tennyson*
Mary Immaculate—*Wordsworth*

Ave Maria — *Scott*
O Maiden Mother — *Tennyson*

Picture Studies: (Perry Picture Company, Malden, Mass.)

Lilies
Sir Galahad — *Watts*
Angel Heads — *Reynolds*
Age of Innocence — *Reynolds*
Infant Samuel — *Reynolds*
Immaculate Conception — *Murillo*

Christ Blessing Children — *Plockhorst*
Innocence — *Eliz. Gardner-Bougereau.*
St. Mary, the Virgin — *Ittenbach*
St. John and the Lamb — *Murillo*

Scripture Texts

O how beautiful is the chaste generation with glory: for the memory thereof is immortal: because it is known both with God and with men. When it is present, they imitate it: and they desire it when it hath withdrawn itself, and it triumpheth crowned forever, winning the reward of undefiled conflicts. *Wisd.* iv. 1, 2.

All uncleanness, let it not so much as be named among you, as becometh saints. *Eph.* v. 3.

---

*The *Mary Book,* published at the Salve Regina Press, Catholic University, Washington, D. C., contains more than eight hundred selections in honor of Mary, many of them by well-known writers.

112

Evil thoughts are an abomination to the Lord. *Prov.* xv. 26.

Many have fallen by the edge of the sword, but not so many as have perished by their own tongue. *Ecclus.* xxviii. 22.

Blessed are the clean of heart, for they shall see God. *Matt.* v. 3–10.

He that loveth cleanness of heart shall have the King for his friend. *Prov.* xxii. 11.

Death comes to the soul through the windows of the eyes. See *Jer.* ix. 21.

In all thy works remember thy last end and thou shalt never sin. *Ecclus.* vii. 40.

The sensual man perceiveth not these things that are of the spirit of God. *Ps.* xxxi. 9.

The impure shall not possess the kingdom of heaven. *I Cor.* vi. 9.

Beware of false prophets, who come to you in the clothing of sheep, but inwardly are ravening wolves! *Matt.* vii. 15.

Out of the abundance of the heart, the mouth speaketh. *Matt.* xii. 34.

He that shall scandalize one of these little ones, that believeth in Me, it were better for him that a millstone be hanged about his neck, and that he should be drowned in the depth of the sea. *Matt.* xviii. 6.

Be holy, because I, the Lord your God, am holy. *Lev.* xix. 2.

Put away filthy speech out of your mouth. *Col.* iii. 8.

Hedge in thy ears with thorns, hear not a wicked tongue, and make doors and bars to thy mouth. *Ecclus.* xxviii. 28.

Know you not that your bodies are the members of Christ? . . . Or know you not that your members are the temples of the Holy Ghost, Who is in you, Whom you have from God; and you are not your own? For you are bought with a great price. Glorify and bear God in your body. *I Cor.* vi. 15–20.

Can a man hide fire in his bosom and his garments not burn? Or can he walk upon hot coals and his feet not be burned? *Prov.* vi. 27, 28.

Quotations and Proverbs

If the candle is to be kept alight, it must be put into a lantern; so if you mean to live chastely, beware of going too much abroad. — *St. Thomas Aquinas.*

An idle brain is the devil's workshop.
Resist the beginning.
The eyes are the windows of the soul.
Idleness is the devil's pillow and the beginning of every vice.
An ounce of prevention is worth a pound of cure.

> She was as good as she was fair.
> None — none on earth above her!
> As pure in thought as angels are,
> To know her was to love her.
> — *Samuel Rogers*

Ambition is the sin of the angels, avarice the sin of men, impurity the sin of the beast. — *St. Bernard.*

To many this seemeth a hard saying: "Deny thyself, take up thy cross, and follow Jesus."
But it will be much harder to hear that last word: "Depart from Me, ye cursed, into everlasting fire. — *Imitation,* Bk. I, chap. xii. 1, 2.
White for purity, red for valor, blue for justice in the flag of our country, to be cherished by all our hearts, to be upheld by all our hands. — *Charles Sumner.*

'Tis one thing to be tempted, another to fall.

> In the fierce unceasing combats
> Let our tranquil war-cry be —
> Omnia pro Te, Cor Jesu! —
> Heart of Jesus, all for Thee!
> — *Rev. M. Russell, S.J.*

Actions, looks, words — steps from the alphabet by which you spell character. — *Lavater.*

It is better to be alone than in bad company. — *George Washington.*

Beautiful faces are those that show
Beautiful thoughts that lie below.

My good blade carves the casques of men,
  My tough lance thrusteth sure,
My strength is as the strength of ten,
  Because my heart is pure.

                   — *Tennyson*

She walks — the lady of my delight —
  A shepherdess of sheep.
Her flocks are thoughts. She keeps them white:
  She guards them from the steep;
She feeds them on the fragrant height,
  And folds them in for sleep.

               — *Alice Meynell*

Whatever you are
You give!
Whatever you think
You live!
So it's wise to think good thoughts,
And kind thoughts, and true,
For whatever you think
You will say and do!

           — *Louise C. Hastings*

Lord for tomorrow and its needs
  I do not pray;
Keep me, my God, from stain of sin
  Just for today.

           — *Sister M. Xavier*

Roses of youth with years fade away,
Bright eyes grow dim, bright locks grow gray;
But there's a flower that will not fade,
A gentle flower that loves the shade —
The graceful lily, pure and sweet,
Of innocence an emblem meet;
This be thy choice in youth's bright day:
Its charms will never pass away.

How great is the charm which innocence lends to a child, to a young girl! So magical is its charm that it often inspires even bad men with awe and veneration. For example, we find the poet Heine, whose own morals were not of the purest, writing these touching lines about an innocent child:

Thou'rt like unto a flower,
  As fair, as pure, as bright.
I gaze on thee and sadness
  Steals o'er my Heart's delight.

I long on those golden tresses
  My folded hands to lay,
Praying that heav'n may preserve thee
  So fair, so pure alway.

To keep thy soul as pure and white
  As lily thou shouldst seek;
And then be sure that roses bright
  Will blossom on thy cheek.

The Vestal Virgins

In heathen Rome six virgins were appointed to keep alive the so-called sacred fire burning on the altar in the temple of Vesta. These virgins usually came to the temple when about ten years of age; they remained there for thirty years, during which time they were forbidden to marry. The Romans held the belief that these virgins brought good fortune to the state, by obtaining for it the protection of the gods. The Vestal Virgins were treated with the greatest respect. Military honors were paid them in public; and if a criminal, on his way to execution, chanced to meet one of them, he was set at liberty. The best places were given them at the theaters and other entertainments at which they might be present. They were clad in white robes, adorned with purple trimming. If one of these virgins broke her vow of chastity, she was condemned to be buried alive. Hence, we see in what high esteem the pagans held those who led a chaste life.

Influence

Because of his great modesty the presence of St. Bernardin alone exerted a good influence over those of his companions who were disorderly. Never feel offended when your companions stop suddenly in the midst of a conversation when you approach; rather feel complimented. Usually it is an uncharitable conversation or one of which they are ashamed; in either case it is best ended. — *Y. C. M.*

The Eyes of God

If we bear in mind that we are in God's presence always and are therefore never alone and unobserved, we are not likely to commit sin. The poet Milton said that he had perpetually before him the thought that he could not escape the eyes of God. — *Y. C. M.*

To a Young Girl

Thou must be holy. Day by day impress
This lesson deeply on thy youthful heart.
Wait not until dark visions of distress
Shall cloud thy light and bid thy joys depart.
Virtue alone can guide to ports of peace.
Virtue alone can teach thee to endure:
This treasure every day and hour increase:
Be virtue thine, the rest is all secure.
— *Selected*

Two Jewels

Lucile had two jewels which she treasured beyond all her possessions. One was purity — the other charity. "I would rather have them than Aunt Alice's diamonds," she assured her Divine Guest after each Holy Communion, and whenever she talked with Him and His Blessed Mother. "I can wear them anywhere and any time of day. Aunt Alice, of course, can't do that with hers. But thieves can steal my jewels just as they can Aunt Alice's, so I have to guard them carefully, all the time. Every time I drive away an impure or uncharitable thought, I give my jewels an extra polishing. I want them to sparkle and be as beautiful as possible. I wouldn't — for anything — trade my jewels for Aunt Alice's diamonds." —*Young Catholic Messenger.*

Books for Reading List

The Pure of Heart, a pamphlet by Rev. Daniel Lord, S.J., The Queen's Work, St. Louis, Mo. May be read by the boys and girls themselves.

A Mother's Letters, Father Alexander, O.F.M., may be obtained through the E. M. Lohmann Co., St. Paul, Minn. This book is excellent for mothers, but can also be placed in the hands of grown-up girls.

Helps to Purity and *Safeguards of Chastity,* written for young women and young men respectively, by Rev. F. Meyer, O.F.M., Frederick Pustet Co., Inc., New York, N. Y.

Educating to Purity, for clergymen, parents, and other educators, by Gatterer and Krus. Frederick Pustet Co.

You and Your Children, by Rev. Paul Hanly Furfey, Ph.D., for parents and educators. Frederick Pustet Co.

The Doctor's Daughter, Life Problems, John's Vacation, and *Chums.* While these booklets are not written from a Catholic point of view, they will aid teachers and parents to instruct their children and to give them a healthy, sensible outlook on life and its problems.

Watchful Elders, for parents and educators, by Rev. Kilian J. Hennrich, O.M.Cap. The Bruce Publishing Company, Milwaukee, Wis.

The Temptation of St. Thomas Aquinas

St. Thomas in his youth wished to embrace the religious state, but his people opposed the idea. They even went so far as to employ a bad woman to make an attempt on his virtue. No sooner had she entered his apartment than the holy youth snatched up a red-hot poker and sent her screaming from the room. Kneeling down then, he thanked God and renewed his vow of perpetual chastity. Soon he fell into a deep sleep, and in a dream beheld two angels approach and bind him about the loins with a cincture. From that time forth he was free from all impure temptations. Every temptation we reject makes us stronger against the next.

An Artist's Answer

King Victor Emanuel requested an Italian sculptor to carve a beautiful statue for him, of the goddess Venus. The artist not only refused to do the work, but sent word to the king that not all the gold and silver in Italy would suffice to tempt him to lay hands to the creation of such a statue. He was too good a Christian to lend his talent to the glorification of paganism and immodesty.

Cardinal Bellarmine and the Paintings

The distinguished prelate, Cardinal Bellarmine, once visited a certain prince. In the antechamber, where he was kept waiting for a long time, there were several paintings of nude figures, which offended against one's sense of modesty and propriety. The Cardinal was very indignant at the sight of these pictures, but when he was admitted to the great man's presence, he did not show his displeasure. Only when his visit was ended he said: "One thing more; may I venture to recommend some people to your Highness, who are in need of even the most necessary garments?" The prince expressed his willingness to comply with the Cardinal's request. As he took his leave in the antechamber, the Cardinal turned, and pointing to the objectionable pictures on the wall, said "Those are the poor creatures of whom I spoke. They are in need of clothing and must have suffered greatly from the cold this winter." The prince smiled, and took the saintly prelate's reproof in good part. The paintings in question were removed from the walls of the antechamber.

The Lily

One of the flowers especially dedicated to "Our Ladie" is the beautiful white lily (Lilium Candidum). It is considered an emblem of purity and beauty, two traits particularly lovable in the Blessed Virgin.

The Lady lily, looking gently down, is almost as much a favorite with poets as the beautiful rose itself, and has generally been regarded as the latter's nearest rival. — *Ave Maria.*

Special Reward of Virgins

St. John (Apoc. xiv. 3, 4) tells us of the special reward of virgins in heaven, for they "follow the Lamb whithersoever He goeth," and sing a song none else can sing. St. John himself for his virginity was especially loved by Christ, Who, when dying upon the cross, gave into the Apostle's keeping His own Virgin Mother.

St. Catherine of Siena

St. Catherine of Siena was once severely tempted against purity, and shortly after our Lord appeared to her. "Where wert Thou, Lord, when those evil thoughts were in my mind?" she said. Jesus smiled and replied, "I was in thy heart, taking pleasure in the victorious battle thou wert waging."

THE EIGHTH COMMANDMENT

The following lesson is so arranged that it can be taught in part, at least, by means of informal discussions. It is understood, of course, that there is no intention of dispensing entirely with the regular classroom procedure or with the Cathechism as a textbook. The Cathechism will serve as a summary and should follow naturally at the end of the lesson.

Not all chapters in the Catechism lend themselves so readily to thorough and free discussion by younger pupils, and not all need as much elaboration. Since, however, the Eighth Commandment is of so great importance to children, and since their attitude toward their schoolwork in particular and toward life in general is so largely conditioned by a thorough knowledge of this Commandment, a method of approach is herewith submitted which will, it is hoped, prove both interesting and effective.

When a small unit of the lesson has been covered, or at any time that the teacher so desires, the work may be varied by dramatization, readings, short stories, etc. Correlation with other subjects will add a great deal to the effectiveness of the work. Especially may this be done with language, history, and citizenship.

Discussion Group

Approach the subject without any reference to the text. If possible, group the children around you in an informal way, as you would for a story hour. Begin by relating some interesting story pertaining to this Commandment, and invite comment and discussion. Have the pupils bring up some of their own problems and let the class help solve them. Gradually submit problems similar to those on the following pages. In each case be sure that a satisfactory conclusion is reached and that the terms are clearly defined. It would be stimulating for the pupils to formulate definitions in their own words, not, indeed, for the purpose of committing them to memory, but for the sake of a clearer understanding of their problems.

Teacher Leads

Success with discussion groups will depend largely, as everywhere else, upon the personality of the teacher. In the first place, the children must have full confidence in her, particularly in her sympathetic understanding of their point of view. Without this attitude on the part of the pupils, the teacher cannot hope to succeed in drawing out the pupils in such a way as to make the discussion profitable to them.

In the second place, the pupils should be encouraged to speak freely of the problems lying within their own experience. It is at such times in particular that the wrong impressions children so frequently have, can be brought to light and corrected. Further, the teacher will do well to direct, rather than impose and to give the pupils every opportunity to add to the store of general information. Reference to the Catechism, the Question Box, and other sources of information should be encouraged. This procedure does not mean giving the pupils too much freedom and allowing them to waste time by idle discussion that has little or no point. Always, the teacher is and must be the guiding force. She must direct, suggest, check, if necessary, and finally draw the discussion to a profitable conclusion. Finally, after a thorough insight into the matter in hand, the children are most likely to be best disposed to apply the lessons learned directly to themselves.

Applying Lesson

If the lessons learned are to be of any benefit to the pupils, they must be applied directly and intelligently for immediate practice. In the case of the Eighth Commandment, for instance, the teacher might ask the pupils to think of the particular fault in themselves which they consider as being most harmful. Not only do they show themselves willing, as a usual thing, but most eager to begin the work of self-knowledge and self-training at once. Such a practice as the following might be assigned: "I will watch very carefully today that I do not act a lie," or, "I shall try to say only good things about others today." In the case of offenses that come to the notice of the teacher, it will be easy for her to give personal direction to the child at fault, and to require an account of the effort made by way of correction.

In order to impress the importance of this work of self-training upon the children, it may be found helpful to add a special prayer after class for the intention of obtaining help in their efforts. For example: "Let us add a little prayer to our Guardian Angel that he may help us speak charitably of others today."

Concrete Problems for Discussion

1. Jack and Bob were neighbors. Bob disliked Jack because the latter had beaten him in a fight. At the beginning of the school year Jack registered in the school which Bob was attending. Now was Bob's chance to get even. He told his classmates that Jack had been expelled from the other school for stealing. The story soon spread over the school.

Suppose the story was true, had Bob a right to talk about it?

What is this sin called?

Suppose the story was not true, what is the sin called?

Jack had been working in the drug store after school hours, in order to help support the family. When the druggist heard the story, he dismissed Jack. What must Bob do to make full satisfaction?

Do you think it is ever possible to retract such a story completely?

Explain to the children why it is almost impossible

to undo the harm resulting from such a lie. People remember the bad things reported more readily than the good things about a person. Besides, people whom Bob does not know will hear the story and brand Jack as a thief. They will probably not hear about the retraction.

If Bob came to you for advice, could you make any suggestions for his overcoming the fault? How would you talk to Bob so as not to hurt his feelings?

2. A friend of yours is passing notes to others and does not pass them to you. You feel sure that she is telling things about you. Are you justified in drawing such conclusions? What sin do you commit?

Can you give other examples of rash judgment?

3. A boy in your class has been found guilty of stealing. A few days later you miss some money out of your desk. You and your classmates conclude that the same boy stole your money. What should you do about it? Discuss fully.

4. Your mother sends you to the door to tell an agent that she is not at home. Should you obey?

Must children obey their parents in all things? Can you give an example of a case in which a child need not obey its parents?

Do you think there is any difference between lies that are harmless and those that are not? What would you consider a harmless lie? A harmful lie?

5. The teacher leaves the classroom and asks all the children to keep on working quietly. As soon as she is out you turn around and laugh and talk. When

she returns you quickly get back to your work. Is there any wrong in that? What would you call such action?

6. Mary knows that Ethel is in bad company and is deceiving her teacher and her parents. Should she tell anyone. Should we always tell when we know something about another person?

7. You have a chance to look into your book during examination. May you do so?

8. The girl sitting behind you in school does not know her lesson. You can help her out by opening your book and placing it so that she can see the lesson. May you help her? Who do you think would be wronged more by such an action, the teacher or the girl?

9. One of the boys in your school is arrested for forgery. Everybody knows about it. May you discuss the matter?

10. You play sick so that you don't have to go to school. Is there any wrong in that?

11. Elsie has a new dress. She asks you how you like it. You do not like it at all, but do not wish to hurt her feelings. How would you answer her?

12. Your friend Margaret tells you a secret and asks you never to tell. You promise. Must you keep your word?

13. Your chum received a letter which she does not show you. You go to her desk later and read the letter without her consent or knowledge. Had you a right to do so?

14. A boy asks you where you are going. You tell him you are going to the North Pole. Is that a lie?

15. You listen with pleasure to an evil story about someone else. Do you commit any wrong?

The Emperor and the Innkeeper

The emperor Rudolph was one day at Nuremberg, and as was the custom at that time, those who had any grievance used to go to him for redress. On this occasion a merchant went to him and reported that, having come into that city on business, he went to one of the chief hotels, and as he had in his possession about two hundred marks of silver in a leather sack, he confided it to the care of the innkeeper during the time he was to remain in his house, that he might put it in a place of safety, but did not ask him for a receipt. When the time came for his departure, he went to the innkeeper and asked him to give him his money, as he was now about to leave the city. The innkeeper looked at him in surprise and declared he had never seen either the sack or the money; and as the merchant had no letter, he found it impossible to prove that he had given him the money. He also informed the emperor that, being one of the chief citizens, the innkeeper had been chosen to be one of the deputation which was to come that day to offer him the homage of the people.

The emperor told the merchant to hide himself somewhere where he might be within call, and that he would see what he could do for him. Not long afterwards the members of the deputation arrived, and the emperor talked familiarly with each of them, inquiring their names and their professions. When he came to the inn-keeper, he said to him in a jocular manner:

"I admire your hat very much; will you give it to me in exchange for mine?"

The innkeeper was only too delighted to do so, thinking that he was indeed highly favored.

Not long afterwards Rudolph left the room, telling the guests to wait till his return. He met one of the officers of his suite near the door and said to him:

"Run as fast as you can to such-and-such an hotel, and tell the landlady to give you immediately the leather sack, which her husband has hidden, for it is much needed at the present time. And as a sign that the case is urgent, show her this hat, and she will immediately recognize it as his."

The officer did as he was commanded, and went to deliver his message. The woman, seeing her husband's hat, and knowing that no one but themselves knew about the stolen money, thought that her husband had sent for it, and gave it to the messenger without any hesitation, who carried it to the emperor. As soon as he received it he returned to the audience chamber and calling to his side the guilty innkeeper, and having also sent for the merchant, he related before the company the whole story. The innkeeper at first answered in indignation that the story was made up to ruin his reputation. Then the emperor, raising up his hand in which was the leather bag, showed it to him and to all those who were present. The innkeeper was struck dumb with astonishment, which was only increased when the emperor related the manner in which the sack had come into his possession. The emperor then gave him a severe reprimand, and ordered him to pay a heavy penalty. — *Chisholm.*

Dramatization

The story "The Emperor and the Innkeeper" can easily be dramatized. Let the children take this and similar stories and write out the dramatization themselves. They will take pleasure in doing it and will, at the same time, derive much profit. Select the play that is considered best by the class and have the pupils stage it during an English class or at some other convenient time. Care should be taken not to make the play too elaborate.

There are many similar stories which will lend themselves easily to dramatization. Not too much of this kind of work should be done, however, in connection with a single chapter of the Catechism. The chief aim should be to bring home to the children those lessons in honesty which come closest to their own problems in daily life.

Stories

There are many stories available in connection with this lesson. It will be necessary, however, to use good judgment in their selection. Again, the teacher should be guided by the close bearing the stories have to the children's own lives. An old story may be more effective when brought up-to-date, put into familiar scenes, and supplied with familiar names.

Short stories could be assigned for the language work. The interest for the children will be greater if they are allowed to give stories of their own selection. The Bible History is rich with incidents pertaining to the Eighth Commandment.

Bulletin Board

Catholic periodicals abound in selections which bring home the lessons taught in the Eighth Commandment. Let the children find such selections themselves and, with the permission of the teacher, post them on a bulletin board in the classroom. Posters, literary selections, memory gems, slogans, etc., all can be brought into play.

The Teacher's Outline

One of the most admirable things that God has given to man is the gift of speech, which distinguishes him from all other creatures. Since the Fall of Adam, this gift has been perverted to many evil uses; for example, calumny, lying, etc. To remedy these evils, God has given us the Eighth Commandment. Our character and reputation are thereby protected. Without these, life, even with all other goods, would be a burden.

"A good name is better than great riches." *Prov.* xxii. 1.

False Witness

I. As in previous Commandments, one sin only is named.

II. But the prohibition includes all such sins as may lead to that one; for example, injustice in thought or word against a neighbor.

III. The Second Commandment forbids words against God: this one, words against our fellow beings.

I. *False Testimony*

1. Giving evidence in a court of justice, which we know to be untrue.
2. Mortal sin, when in a serious matter, whether for or against an accused person, because:
   a) Grievous violation:
      Of a solemn public trust.
      Of justice.
   b) The injustice is often beyond repair.
   c) Public disgrace often attaches to the family also of a perjurer.
3. Contains a threefold guilt:
   a) Falsehood against the truth.
   b) Perjury, in breaking the oath.
   c) Injustice, by the injury it causes.
4. Contains a threefold offense against:
   a) God, by contempt in His presence.
   b) The judge, by deception.
   c) Society, condemning a just member, or releasing a villain.

5. Hateful to God:
"A false witness shall not be unpunished."
Prov. xix. 5.
6. Usually given through:
   a) Fear, when a witness is intimidated.
   b) Love, when a friend is questioned.
   c) Interest, when a bribe is offered.
   d) Malice, when hatred leads to false evidence.
7. Involves the duty of repairing the evil done to another's honor, etc.
   Hence, in court, always speak the truth, whatever be the consequences.

II. *Rash Judgment*

1. Assent of the will to suspicions about others, without sufficient grounds.
2. Opposed to:
   a) Justice; each one has a right to his good name until really forfeited.
   b) Charity, which "thinketh no evil" and obliges us to love others as ourselves.
3. We may be guilty of it by:
   a) Conceiving dislikes at first sight.
   b) Attributing the acts of others to bad motives.
   c) Judging a person addicted to sin because once guilty of it.
   d) Pronouncing one guilty without hearing his defense.

4. Guilt seen thus:
   a) Christ expressly forbids it.
   b) It shows corruption of heart, they judging most who are guilty.
   c) It generally arises from pride usurping authority to judge.
   d) Often from envy and hatred — Behavior of the Pharisees to Our Lord.
   e) Most injurious to a neighbor, depriving him unjustly of his reputation in our mind.
   f) It produces such evil results: hatred and bloodshed.
   g) Sometimes punished even in this world.
5. It is easy to be deceived in passing judgment. Our own past experience will verify this. Take care, therefore, in judging others to take always the charitable view.

III. *Lies*

1. Words or signs against the truth, to deceive a neighbor.
2. The devil told the first lie in Eden, hence called the "father of lies."
3. Especially hateful to God, the "God of truth."
4. To say an untruth, believing it a truth is not a lie, but an error.
5. Kinds of lies:
   a) Jocose lie: spoken to please and hurting no one.

b) Officious lie: hurting no one, but intended to be of service; lie of excuse.

c) Malicious lie: injurious to God and man.

d) Sacrilegious lie: profanation of the Sacrament. Concealing a mortal sin in confession.

e) Hypocrisy: putting on the appearance only of holiness.

f) Flattery: praising beyond the truth. —Assuring the dying there is no danger of death.

6. Guilt of lies:

   a) Every lie is a sin, mortal or venial, according to its nature.

   b) Hence it is never lawful to lie, no matter for what object.

7. Conceive a great horror of lies, because:

   a) A lie is an abuse of God's most admirable gift, speech.

   b) A lie is an attack on God Who is Truth itself.

   c) A lie dishonors him who tells it.

8. Hence the need of watchfulness in parents, as to truthfulness of children.

9. Mental reservations and equivocations, when unlawfully deceptive, are sinful.

10. But we may hide the truth without being guilty of lying.

Calumny, Detraction, Etc.

I. *Calumny*

 1. Man has three lives, namely:
     a) The corporal life of the body, injured and lost by wounding, etc.
     b) The spiritual life of grace, injured and destroyed by sin.
     c) The civil life of good fame, injured and ruined by calumny, etc.
 2. Imputing crimes and faults to others untruly. Whether to individuals or communities.
     a) By word of mouth, by letter, or by action.
     b) Whether through malice or interest.
 3. Exaggerating real faults and defects.
 4. Denying others' good qualities or actions.
 5. Most odious and malicious sin. Yet how common, especially in moments of passion.
 6. Calumny is a sin against:
     a) Truth: Saying knowingly what is absolutely false.
     b) Charity: showing absence of love and destroying peace of families.
     c) Justice: endangering the prospects of the victim and his family.
     d) Religion: which cannot exist where the tongue is not bridled.
     e) Manly courage: stabbing in the dark, without giving a chance of defense.

7. Guilt of calumny:
   a) Always a sin because always a lie.
   b) Shown from Scripture:
      "Thou shalt not calumniate thy neighbor." *Lev.* xix. 13.
   c) Will vary according to:
      The nature of the imputation made.
      The injury intended or effected.
      The number of persons hearing it.
   d) A most cruel persecution:
      Its bitterness penetrates most deeply the soul.
      In other trials there is usually some alleviation, seldom in this.
      Job bore many things in patience, but justified himself in calumny.
      Hence the magnificent reward promised:
      "Be glad and rejoice, for your reward is very great in heaven." *Matt.* v. 12.
8. Source of terrible evils, for example:
   a) Dissensions and discord.
   b) Hatred and bloodshed.
   c) Temporal losses and misfortunes.
   d) Eternal ruin of souls.

II. *Detraction*

1. Making known without cause, the secret faults of others. By word of mouth, insinuation, silence, writing, etc.

2. Imparting uncharitable news even as a secret.
3. Hinting that there are things others do not know of a neighbor.
4. Praising coldly, so as to insinuate him undeserving.
5. Seeking to lessen the merit of his good acts.
6. Detraction is a sin:
   a) As seen from the word of God: "Thou shalt not be a detractor nor a whisperer among the people." *Lev.* xix. 16.
   b) Against Charity:
   Exercising an act of hatred or dislike against a neighbor.
   Exposing him to the contempt and ridicule of others.
   Diminishing esteem for him in those who listen.
   Causing him pain should it reach his ears.
   c) Against Justice:
   Robbing him of the esteem others may have for him.
   Exposing him thereby to temporal loss (trade, profession, etc.).
   d) Against the example of Christ, Who would not name the one about to betray Him.
   e) Committing almost a threefold murder in:
   The detractor's own soul, because he sins.
   The soul of the listener who is also guilty.
   The civil life of the one of whom evil is spoken.

7. Guilt of detraction depends on:
   a) The person who speaks (character and position).
   b) The person spoken of (superior, consecrated to God).
   c) The nature of the fault revealed (lying, drunkenness).
   d) In some cases the number of persons to whom it is made known (although only one sin is committed).
   e) Injury done or foreseen.
8. Forbidden also in regard to the dead (also calumny):
   a) Though departed they still have a right to their good name.
   b) The surviving friends are also affected by the detraction.
   c) It may sometimes be even a mortal sin.
9. We have faults enough of our own without troubling about those of others.
10. Source of many evils (like calumny); for example:
    a) Hatred and revenge.
    b) Misunderstandings and suspicions.
    c) Temporal losses.
    d) Eternal ruin.
11. Lawful sometimes to reveal the faults of others.
    a) When for their good (their correction). Informing parents of the evil ways of their children.

b) When necessary in order to prevent greater evil.

Saying the truth to persons engaging servants, lending money.

Justifying one's self from a crime.

c) When accompanied with the necessary conditions.

Through pure motive only.

Revealing only to those who can remedy the evil.

Without exaggerating the fault.

III. *Talebearing*

1. Repeating to anyone what others have said to him; for example: servant about master, neighbor about neighbor.
2. Sinful because:
   a) Opposed to the word of God.

   "The talebearer shall defile his own soul." *Ecclus.* xxi. 31.

   b) Source of quarrels and animosities.

   c) Cause of misunderstanding and loss of friendship.
3. Guilt will depend upon:
   a) The intention of the speaker.

   b) The injury done or foreseen.
4. Lawful revealing is not talebearing.

IV. *Words which injure our neighbor's character*

For example:

1. Backbiting:

a) Opposed to the law of Christian charity.

b) How common when people meet together.

c) Honest criticism may be lawful, but must guard against personalities and uncharitableness.

2. Contumely:

    a) Raillery and insults offered to a person's face, nicknames, sarcasm.

    b) Words of reproach as to some sin, failure, or misfortune.

    c) Actions: as destroying a photo or statue, through contempt.

    d) May sometimes be a grievous sin.

V. *Listening willingly to calumny, etc., also forbidden*

1. Directly or indirectly:

    a) Encouraging it, by showing interest, asking questions.

    b) Hearing with pleasure.

    c) Not preventing it when able.

2. Guilt of listening:

    a) Will vary, as calumny and detraction.

    b) May include scandal by consent, etc. If there were no listeners there would be no detractors.

    c) May depend:
    On the duty of a listener; for example, a superior.

On the motive; for example, curiosity, malice.

d) "The detractor and the listener both have the devil in them: one in his mouth, the other in his ears." — *St. Bernard.*

3. Conduct in presence of calumny, etc.

a) If a superior is guilty, show displeasure by the countenance.

b) If an equal, turn the conversation, say something good of the injured.

c) If an inferior, reprove him and impose silence.

d) If the conversation continues, show displeasure at least by silence.

e) If this avail not, leave the company rather than sin with them.

VI. *Betraying secrets forbidden by this same Commandment*

1. Sinful, unless for grave reasons:
2. Kinds of secrets:

a) Simple: when we happen to know what we feel should be kept secret.

b) Intrusted: given on the condition, at least implied, that we keep it. For example, professional knowledge of doctors, lawyers.

c) Promised: When we are asked and we promise to keep it.

d) Secret got by fraud, for example:
   By listening to conversation.
   By prying into drawers, boxes, etc.
   By reading other person's letters. Which
   may sometimes be even a mortal sin.
3. Unworthy of a generous nature, still more of
   a Christian.
4. Guilt of revealing secrets will depend on:
   a) Importance of the secret.
   b) The injury likely to follow.
5. Resist the beginnings of curiosity and go out
   of the way of temptation.
6. May sometimes be lawful, for example:
   a) When the matter is trifling and no injury
      is feared.
   b) When consent may reasonably be pre-
      sumed.
   c) When there is good and reasonable cause,
      good of the state, defense of the innocent.
   d) Never lawful in the case of the seal of
      confession.

VII. *To make satisfaction*

1. Positive obligation, often most difficult, yet
   strictly binding.
2. If it can be made, pardon for sin cannot be
   had without it.
3. Hence, who so injures another, by speaking
   ill of him, must repair the evil as far as he
   can.

4. It must be done without delay, or the evil may only increase.

VIII. *By restoring good name*

1. In false testimony, for example, should a man be sent to prison, the perjurer is bound:
   a) To restore the prisoner's character.
   b) To obtain his release, if possible.
   c) To provide meanwhile for his family.
   d) To repair the consequent evils.
2. In Rash Judgment: To correct in one's mind and the minds of others the evil opinions held or given of a neighbor.
3. In Calumny: The false accusation must be absolutely denied.
4. In Detraction: The statement cannot be withdrawn because true, but,
   a) Excuse the person, if the case admit it.
   b) Excuse at least the motives or intention.
   c) Allow for violence of temptation, difficult circumstances, etc.
   d) Speak of the neighbor's good deeds, qualities, etc.
5. In Contumely: according to the:
   a) Nature of the offense: a blow or an insult.
   b) Position of the one offending.
      If a superior be at fault, some act of kindness will usually suffice.
      If an equal, beg pardon and apologize.

If an inferior, it may be necessary to do
so on bended knee, and perhaps in public.

  c) Disposition of the offender:
Some would not feel asking pardon, even
on their knees.

6. See the evil of sins of the tongue, and the
obligations they entail.
7. In opposition to such sins endeavor always:
   a) To entertain kind thoughts of others, as
   a remedy for suspicion.
   b) To put kind interpretations on their acts,
   against rash judgments.
   c) To speak kind words, instead of those
   that wound and injure.

IX. *Social advantages of the Eighth Commandment*

1. The tongue is the chief instrument of the
iniquities of the earth.
2. These are fertile sources of trouble and
sorrow to society.
3. To remedy them, God has given this Commandment:
   a) Safeguarding our honor and character.
   b) Clearing society of suspicions, etc., which
   makes men devils.
   c) Restoring truth, etc., which makes an
   anticipated heaven.
4. Thus there is not one of our interests that
God in His goodness does not surround with
a sacred barrier.

Scripture Texts

A good name is better than riches. *Prov.* xxii. 1.

A false witness shall not be unpunished. *Prov.* xix. 5.

A false witness shall perish. *Prov.* xxi. 28.

A man that beareth false witness against his neighbor, is like a dart and a sword. *Prov.* xxv. 18.

Rash Judgment

Judge not, that you may not be judged. *Matt.* vii. 1.

But who art thou that judgest thy neighbor? *Jas.* iv. 13.

Is thy eye evil, because I am good? *Matt.* xx. 15.

Lies

Lying lips are an abomination to the Lord. *Prov.* xii. 22.

Be not willing to make any manner of lie. *Ecclus.* vii. 14.

Lie not one to another. *Col.* iii. 9.

A lie is a foul blot in a man. *Ecclus.* xx. 26.

Calumny

Thou shalt not calumniate thy neighbor. *Lev.* xiv. 13.

The poison of asps is under their lips. *Ps.* xiii. 3.

They have whetted their tongues like a sword. *Ps.* lxiii. 4.

Their tongue is a piercing arrow, it hath spoken deceit. *Jer.* ix. 8.

Reward: Be glad and rejoice, for your reward is very
great in heaven. *Matt.* v. 12.

Detraction

His words are smoother than oil, and the same are
darts. *Ps.* liv. 22.

Thou shalt not be a detractor nor a whisperer among
the people. *Lev.* xix. 16.

The detractor is the abomination of men. *Prov.*
xxiv. 9.

Hast thou heard a word against thy neighbor? let it
die within thee. *Ecclus.* xix. 10.

Detractors, hateful to God. *Rom.* i. 30.

Detract not one another, my brethren. *Jas.* iv. 11.

Talebearing

The talebearer shall defile his own soul. *Ecclus.*
xxi. 31.

The whisperer . . . hath troubled many that were at
peace. *Ecclus.* xxviii. 15.

The tongue of a third person hath disquieted many.
Ecclus. xxviii. 16.

The talebearer . . . shall be hated by all. *Ecclus.*
xxi. 31.

Backbiting, Contumely, Listening, Etc.

If a serpent bite in silence, he is nothing better that
backbiteth secretly. *Eccles.* x. 11.

Whosoever shall say, thou fool, shall be in danger of
hell-fire. *Matt.* v. 22.

Have nothing to do with detractors. *Prov.* xxiv. 21.

Hedge in thy ears with thorns, hear not a wicked tongue. *Ecclus.* xxviii. 28.

Worthy of death . . . they also that consent to them. *Rom.* i. 32.

The tongue is a fire, a world of iniquity. *Jas.* iii. 6.

An unquiet evil, full of deadly poison. *Jas.* iii. 8.

By it we bless God, and by it we curse men. *Jas.* iii. 9.

Biblical References

False Testimony

Achab against Naboth. *III Kings* xxi. 13.

The two Elders against Susanna. *Dan.* xiii. 61.

The Jews accusing our Lord of blasphemy. *Matt.* xxvi. 61.

Rash Judgment

Eliphaz and Job. *Job.* iv. 7.

Putiphar thought his wife's accusation proof of guilt. *Gen.* xxxix. 19.

Benjamin and the cup. *Gen.* xliv.

Judith adorning herself to go to Holofernes. *Jth.* x. 4.

The Pharisee against Mary Magdalen. *Luke* vii. 39.

The Pharisee against the Publican. *Luke* xviii. 2.

The Barbarians against St. Paul. *Acts* xxviii. 4.

Lies

The devil told the first lie in Eden, hence called the "father of lies." *John* viii. 44.

Sarah saying she did not laugh. *Gen.* xviii. 15.
The devil speaking to Eve. *Gen.* iii. 4.
Jacob to Isaac. *Gen.* xxvii. 24.
The woman before Solomon. *III Kings* iii. 20.
The scribes at the Resurrection. *Matt.* xxviii. 13.

Hypocrisy

Herod and the Magi. *Matt.* ii. 8.
Judas at the Last Supper. *Matt.* xxvi. 25.

Flattery

Acclamation of the people to Herod. *Acts* xii. 22.
The Pharisees seek to ensnare Jesus in His speech.
  Matt. xxii. 15–21.

Calumny

Putiphar's Wife. *Gen.* xxxix. 14.
The Pharisees and Our Lord. *Matt.* xii. 24.
The Chief Priests and the Apostles. *Matt.* xxviii. 13.
Aman's Calumny punished. *Esther* xvi. 18.
Joseph's imprisonment. *Gen.* xxxix. 20.
Job justified his calumny. *Job* xxxi.

Contumely

The friends of Tobias. *Tob.* ii. 15.
The wife of Job. *Job* ii. 9.

SEVENTH AND TENTH COMMANDMENTS[1]

In presenting the Seventh and Tenth Commandments as the basis for study, it is well to draw attention to the fact that both are violations of justice. The Seventh Commandment forbids the external actions while the Tenth points out intentions and desires against the virtue of justice. In the Seventh Commandment, God commands us to respect our neighbor's property and all his rights. We must give to all men what belongs to them. We may neither damage their property nor practice fraud or deceit. We must render them justice.

In the Tenth Commandment, God takes even greater precaution for our protection in that He commands the respect of property in our hearts. We may not desire our neighbor's property unjustly nor be envious of his possessions. In the *Sacred Heart Messenger,* April, 1929, "Tommy's Divine Chum," by G. Cain; "Mrs. Delafield's Goose," by V. Jones; and "Blessed Are the Poor," by Giles Black, O.P., are fine stories for the introductory lesson.[2]

Introductory Questions

1. Mother has given you a dollar to procure groceries. The sale today saves you ten cents. What will a

---

[1]For grades 5 and 6.   2 These stories can be found in the appendix, p. 171.

truly honest boy do? What do you say about the boy who would spend it for candy without his mother's knowledge?

2. What would you say about putting that money into the mite box in school without your mother's knowledge?

3. Even though stealing a pencil or some paper from a friend is not a serious sin, still you know that it is wrong. Why should you not take it? (It offends God venially.)

4. What do you think will happen to a child who has the habit of taking little things from his neighbor in school without asking his permission?

5. If you know that a certain girl is taking things from the other pupils, will you keep still about it as long as your things are not taken? Whom should you tell?

6. Tell the children what you would say, Mary, to a little girl in your class who took your pencils a number of times and has not returned them.

7. You know your little friend has taken a quarter from his home and bought some candy. He offers to treat you. Are you stealing by taking some of it? How would you make him realize that this is very wrong?

8. You read so often or hear frequently about robberies especially in the large cities. What is robbery and what kind of sin is it?

9. What is the difference between robbery and theft?

10. This last Christmas robbers broke into an

orphanage in St. Paul and stole the orphans' gifts and goodies, even some of their clothes. Did they commit a graver sin than if they had stolen from other children?

11. If a person is really starving and freezing, is he permitted to take the necessary eatables or clothing?

12. What kind of sin is it to steal from the Church, something that belongs to the Church? (Sacrilege.) Is it always a mortal sin? (No.)

13. Very frequently when people go traveling, they will take towels, napkins, spoons, and such like, as souvenirs from places they visit. Is this stealing?

14. A boy worked for some people on Saturdays. Among his different jobs, he also carried wood into the cellar. He helped himself to apples he saw there, continually. Fifteen years later he returned to the people and gave them ten dollars for what he had pilfered in his youth. What do you think of him for doing that?

Justice

1. I know a boy of about 16 who is working on a farm so as to earn his way through high school. Very often the farmer keeps the boy from school for work. How is the man failing against justice?

2. Just a few years ago many babies died in New York. It was proved that the milk which the mothers bought for them was not pure and nutritious enough. It had been adulterated and so the mothers were cheated. Who is guilty before God for so many deaths?

3. A merchant has been using incorrect weights for defrauding the people. What can you say about such methods?

4. You have a counterfeit dollar and know it. You got it from somebody else in change. You will be the loser if you do not use it to pay your debt. What will you do in the case?

5. The conductor has forgotten to collect your fare. Should you pay him of your own accord?

6. Many men make money by gambling. They are Catholics and go to Church regularly. What might Protestants say on this point about the Catholic Church? What do you say?

7. Mr. Frank is always grumbling about paying his school taxes and assessments, saying he has no children in school. Why do you think he is doing wrong?

8. In a very famous letter to the world, called an encyclical, Pope Leo XIII, Our Holy Father, said, "Every wage earner is entitled to a just wage." What do you think he meant? Explain also how the wage earner must be just to his employer.

9. Whenever you have found something of great or small value, what does the Church order you to do? When would it be impossible to fulfill the command of the Church and what must you do then?

10. A boy, who was considered a simpleton, entered a skiing contest. He won the first prize, but the men would not give it to him. What do you say about this?

11. Your older brothers are earning money. They

do not help pay the family expenses, although they are still staying at home. Has your father the right to make them pay board and room?

12. Some day when you have people working for you, how are you going to treat them?

On Coveting Our Neighbor's Goods

(For coveting my neighbor's goods sinfully, it is necessary not only to desire to have the *same* goods as my neighbor, but I must also wish him to be deprived of them. — *Christian Doctrine,* DeZulueta, S.J.)

1. A poor boy wishes to have a good suit of clothes like that of his wealthier friend. The mere wishing is not a sin. How would it become one? (He would do wrong in desiring the identical suit to deprive his friend of it.)

2. You and another little boy have been striving to win the highest honors in class. Both of you have worked very, very hard. He wins. A temptation to wish him all kinds of bad things comes upon you, but you heroically overcome it and are kind and good to him. Who is the greater hero in God's eyes?

3. How do you think a child will grow up who is never satisfied with what he has but always wants more and more?

4. When you are tempted to desire something unlawfully, how about thinking like this: "No person knows my thoughts, but there is One who examines my mind and heart — God."

5. Does the Tenth Commandment forbid one to desire great advancement in one's work or in acquiring property?

On Respecting Our Neighbor's Property

1. John has cut a little hole in his school desk. Day by day it gets a little larger. Is he committing sin?

2. You see a boy marking up some of the school books with ink. What are you going to do about that, or isn't it any of your business?

3. On your way home from school every evening a group of boys does something wrong and thinks it a good joke; for instance, they mark up or smear walls of buildings, steal fruit from a stand or from an orchard, tear each other's clothing, break down fences. You know all these things are wrong — what could you do about it?

4. At times a child is found in school who is happy when he can damage property. He lets the faucet open, writes on the walls, breaks locks, etc. How could you other boys help him to stop this?

5. Your neighbor is always asking you for paper, pencils, ink; you seem to supply him continually. Your parents are not giving you money for him. How must you respect the money your parents give you?

6. Are you helping that child to become a good, reliable man by continually giving him what he should himself provide?

7. You have borrowed a book from your friend. Of course, you mean to restore it, but months have slipped

by and the book is showing pretty hard use. How are you failing in showing respect to your neighbor's property?

8. You have kept the book so long and it looks so shabby that you are ashamed to return it and so you just naturally forget about it. Aren't you committing sin?

9. A common saying is that public property is nobody's property. What obligations have you toward any public property?

Cooperating in Injustice

1. *Command:* I know your good parents would never command you to steal anything. There are some poor little children whose parents teach them to steal. They even command them under pain of punishment to take food or money whenever they have a chance. Who is committing a very grievous sin? Is the child to be blamed at all? What might he try to tell them?

2. *Counsel:* A child says to you, "Tell your father you need 50 cents for a new book. I'll tell mine the same. Then we'll go to the show and buy some ice cream." What will an honorable child say to him?

3. *Praise:* A boy on his way home from school often teases an old man by throwing stones at his dog or his house. You are with him one evening when he does it. Instead of committing sin with him by praising him, what will you say to him?

4. *Recourse:* You know that the police are after a bootlegger. Once upon a time your father was helped

by this man. May your father, in return for this former act of charity, now conceal him in your home?

5. *Partaking:* Your little sister has stolen four doughnuts from the pantry. You catch her eating them. She gives you two. What should you do?

6. *Nonpreventing:* You hear two boys using very profane language. You know they will stop a little anyway if you tell them, but you think it is no affair of yours. How far are you guilty?

7. *Silence:* In No. 5, you do not accept the doughnuts, but you do not tell her that she is doing wrong. Are you guilty of sin?

8. *Not making known:* A girl has stolen a fountain pen. You know she has it but you will not tell on her. What would be the honorable way of acting on your part?

On the Obligation of Restitution

There are three points, dear children, which you must ever keep before your mind in reference to these Commandments: (*a*) ill-gotten goods must be restored to their rightful owners; (*b*) injury done to our neighbor's property must be repaired as far and as soon as we are able; (*c*) we cannot receive absolution in confession under any other conditions.

1. Even in small matters, children, you must make restitution. Why do you think this is so necessary?

2. You have stolen apples and eaten them. How would you make restitution?

3. You have borrowed paper, ink, pencils, so often.

Of course you asked your friends, but did you ever really think that you have taken things their parents have bought for them? Are you obliged to restore their value?

4. In school a child has again and again stolen small sums of money. He does not know any more from whom he has taken them nor how much from each one. He wants to begin to live decently again. How can he go about making restitution to all concerned?

5. So frequently people neglect to pay their hospital bills, private nurses, medicines. To what is a Catholic strictly bound in this matter?

6. You have taken money from home. Are you obliged to restore it to your parents? How will you do it?

7. You have used someone's book so long that it has become ragged. Are you obliged to get him another?

8. Since you are still a very little child, you cannot earn money to restore what you have taken, to pay what you have broken. What are you going to do about it?

9. You are afraid to tell this to your parents. How could you become a real trustworthy child again?

10. You are about twelve years old. When you were eight, you purposely threw stones and broke some windows. You never told anybody, but now you are worried about it. What will you do?

11. A merchant has become rich through wrong dealings, selling things for more than they are worth,

giving wrong change to children. How is he to make restitution?

12. A man defrauded the people when he was cashier of a bank. Bankruptcy resulted. Meanwhile he has increased his own wealth on the money which he used illegally. How much must he restore if he wishes to save his soul? (Principal plus interest.)

13. In No. 12, the man will lose his good name if he restores it in person. Is he obliged to do it that way?

14. A man has charged high interest (usury). People simply had to borrow his money and he took advantage. Must he restore any to the people?

15. The man from whom another has stolen a large amount of money has died. To whom must the money and the interest be restored?

16. If there are no heirs, can the thief simply give it to the Church or to the poor as he pleases?

17. I know a family who runs high bills in all stores. Bills come continually which they disregard until the law gets after them. Why is such action wrong?

18. Is it wrong for renters not to pay rent regularly, especially if the owner depends upon this money for his living?

19. A public officer has defrauded the state of thousands of dollars. If he returns it, he will be poverty-stricken and also his family. What is the law of the Church in his regard?

20. What would you rather, live to be eighty years old, a millionaire, (through ill-gotten money) honored

and esteemed on earth, then after death suffer a hell for never-ending ages; or be honestly poor and enjoy a heaven for never-ending ages? "What shall it profit a man, if he gain the whole world, and suffer the loss of his soul?"— Mark viii, 36.

A Story, Sad, but Alas! too True

A young man who lived in a populous part of the country had contracted in his childhood a habit of stealing. At first it was but small things. Sometimes he stole bread and fruit and nuts in his father's house. But when he grew a little older, he found his way into the gardens of his neighbors and stole fruit and vegetables. At length he became more daring, and began to steal money in small sums from his parents, and any other thing he took a fancy to, which fell under his hands.

He next tried to steal from his companions and his neighbors, and, on account of his cunning, succeeded in escaping without even being suspected.

It is true he often heard of the penalties that were inflicted on robbers when they were discovered — that some of them were imprisoned, made to endure hard labor, and that many even were put to death on the scaffold. Although he dreaded all these things, he hoped that his cleverness would make him escape them in the future, as it had done until then. Thus he continued his evil life and with such success that, although he had already plundered much and had stolen even very valuable things, he had not once been suspected. At length he began to think that all the stories he had heard about robbers and their dismal ends were invented to frighten him.

With this idea and taking his past successes as the measure of those yet to come, he boldly undertook still greater enterprises. He chose a certain number of young men, as wicked as he himself was, and formed a gang which infested the whole neighborhood. Over and over again had the men kept up the appearance of piety and no one suspected them.

But the prosperity of the wicked generally comes to an untimely end. One night, as they were engaged in their evil work, it happened that a man who belonged to that part of the country was returning home late, and met the robbers as they were going to the place where they concealed their booty. They had stolen a great quantity and each had a heavy load. The man, who knew them, was surprised at seeing them out so late, and knew that they must have been engaged in stealing. They, too, seeing that they were discovered at last, and that if they allowed him to escape, he would inform upon them, and that their career would thus be brought to an end, resolved to murder him. This they therefore did, and left his body on the roadside.

When this murder was discovered, great consternation filled the whole county. The magistrates sent out armed men to apprehend, if possible, the murderers, and they suceeded, in course of time, in arresting them. When they were brought to trial, it soon became known that they were also the robbers who had stolen so much other property, for some of the stolen goods were found in their possession.

At the end of the trial, being found guilty, they were condemned to die on the scaffold. A terrible warning was this to all who heard the history of the unfortunate young man, who had begun his career by taking away what was in itself of but little consequence, and had ended it by the terrible crime of murder.

Francis Egan, the Honest Shop Boy

In a certain great manufacturing city, a youth named Francis Egan, who had recently left college, where he had been instructed in the true principles of a Christian life, had obtained a position of clerk in the office of a rich manufacturer. He was energetic and willing, and soon won the confidence of his employer.

One day a letter came recalling an order for goods. The merchant handed the letter to Francis, and with a smile said: "Francis, write an answer to this letter, and say that the goods were shipped before the letter countermanding the order came to hand."

Francis looked into the face of his employer with a sad but firm glance, and replied: "I cannot do that, sir."

"Why not?" asked the merchant angrily.

"Because that is not the truth, for you know that the goods are still here in the shop, and it would be a lie to write what you ask me."

"I hope you will always be as particular," replied the merchant, turning on his heels and going away.

Did Francis lose his place? No! The merchant, although angry at the time, knew from these words the value of the lad. He not only kept him in his office, but soon raised him to the position of the confidential clerk.

Months and years went on, and Francis, by his honesty and his attention to the affairs of his master, made himself very valuable to him, and after ten years' service he was admitted as a partner in the firm, and is now one of the richest men in New York.

Honesty will pay both in this life and in the next. — *The Chimes.*

The Temptation of the Two Brothers

Two noble knights were one day passing together through a thick forest on their way to a tournament. They were brothers, and each of them possessed great riches.

As they were passing through this solitary place, the demon

161

of covetousness inspired both of them with the same wicked thought — that of killing his brother, in order to obtain his share of wealth.

But, as they were Christians, and feared to offend God, they both resisted the temptation; but still their consciences were not at rest. So when they reached the nearest village, the one said to the other: "I am going to look for a priest, for I want to go to confession."

The other one answered: "I also have the same desire." So they went to the church and made their confession.

After both had finished, and were about to continue their journey, one of them said to the other: "My dear brother, I must tell you of a terrible temptation that came into my mind when we were passing through the forest. Satan tempted me to take away your life, that I might obtain possession of your wealth."

The other brother started back in surprise. "My brother, the same thought also came into my mind, and I was tempted to kill you, that I might become possessed of your property; but I, too, banished the temptation."

This revelation filled them both with such a horror of wealth, which so nearly was the cause of crime, that on the spot they resolved to renounce forever the riches of this world, so dangerous in time and for eternity, and went to live together in a hut which they built for themselves in a forest.

Thus was begun the famous monastery in the forest of Molesme, in the middle of the eleventh century. — *Lives of the Saints*, March 28.

The Rich Merchant on His Deathbed

A certain merchant, who was very rich, fell dangerously ill. His friends, perceiving that his malady was likely to be fatal, exhorted him to enter into himself, and prepare to appear before God. He promised to do so, but deferred the execution of his promise from day to day.

Several learned and prudent confessors were recommended to him, but the sick man, under various pretexts, refused to see them.

In the meantime a certain missionary of great renown for sanctity happened to pass through the town. The merchant, being informed of it, and conscious that his end was drawing near, consented to receive him.

The missionary inspired him with confidence, so he opened his heart to him, and said: "Father, my conscience has been for a length of time much troubled respecting many things connected with my business."

"Be pleased," answered the missionary, "to let me know the cause of your uneasiness and doubts."

The penitent immediately began, but after explaining one or two points, his ideas suddenly became confused, and the remainder of his discourse was totally disconnected. The confessor was greatly embarrassed. "If I propose to him any questions," thought he, "I shall only increase the confusion of his mind." In this perplexity he determined not to interrupt the penitent, and while the latter continued to speak, he fervently besought the Almighty to direct him as to the best means of promoting the salvation of his soul.

The rich man having ceased, the confessor waited a little while that his mind might become somewhat composed, which happily took place soon after. Then, addressing his penitent, he said: "My dear friend, you are a man distinguished for intelligence and prudence in the management of commercial affairs; moreover, you are gifted with a fair and upright mind. If one of your friends should, on his deathbed, consult you upon the case which you have just proposed to me, what would you answer?"

"I would tell him," said the sick man, "that he should make

163

unconditional restitution. Things now appear to me in a far different light from that in which I formerly viewed them."

"Well, my good friend," replied the confessor, "adopt in your own case the same measure which you would recommend to another. The eternal reward which awaits you in heaven is infinitely more precious than all the riches of this world."

The merchant profited by this salutary advice, and, sending for a notary, caused a formal declaration, agreeable to the dictates of his conscience, to be drawn up. He then, with the assistance of the missionary, made a humble confession; but no sooner had he ended than the light of reason, which heaven had afforded him, became suddenly eclipsed, and he heaved his last sigh in the arms of his confessor.

The Hermit's Barley Field

In the year 1757, during the Seven Years' War between Frederick the Great, King of Prussia, and other European powers, it happened that a cavalry officer was commissioned to go forth on a foraging expedition in one of the provinces occupied by the troops.

When he reached a certain valley where he had expected to find much corn, he discovered that the whole country, as far as his eyes could see, was barren and uncultivated. He was about to return to camp, when he saw a hut almost hidden in the dense foliage of a thicket not far from the rough path on which he rode.

Going up to the door, he knocked, and it was opened by a hermit, whose hair and beard showed that he had reached the evening of life.

"My Father," said the officer, "could you point out to me any place where I might be able to procure provisions for our horses?"

The old man informed him that at some distance there

was a field of barley, and offered his services to accompany him and his men, and point it out to them.

When they had proceeded about the distance of a mile, they came to a field on which was growing a magnificent crop of the barley.

"Ah," cried the officer, "this must be the place."

"No, sir," replied the hermit, "the field to which I am leading you is still at a little distance, but we shall soon reach it."

About a mile farther on they came to another field, covered with the ripened grain, but not so luxuriant as the one they had passed. Here the hermit stopped, and pointing to it, said: "This is the field."

The men dismounted and cut down the ripe crops; then, binding it in large bundles, placed them upon their horses, and returned.

When they were passing near the other field, the officer thus accosted the hermit: "My Father, you have made us take a useless journey in bringing us so far, when here, much nearer to your abode, is a field even more abundant than the one you brought us to."

"Yes, sir," replied the old man, "the barley in this field is certainly better than that which you have taken; but this field belongs to someone else, whereas the field you have harvested belongs to me."

The officer, struck with astonishment at these words, and filled with admiration for the pious old man, uncovered his head, and bowed it toward him in token of his profound respect. He had observed with scrupulous exactness during his whole life, every point of honor exacted by his position, but he had never before seen an example of such admirable disinterestedness displayed by those among whom his rank caused him to be associated. "This is indeed the sublime fruit which the love of God and of His law produces," he said, "in the heart of those who love God and serve Him perfectly."

Other interesting stories are: St. Eligius, the Goldsmith (*Legend of the Saints*); A Witness from the Grave (*Life of St. Stanislaus*) May 7; St. Francis of Assissi (Oct. 4) ;Blessed Herman Joseph; St. Elizabeth of Hungary; St. Nicholas.

Bible Stories

1. Selling of Joseph
2. Joseph's Silver Cup
3. Job, Deprived of his Property
4. Aachen
5. Pharaoh and his Punishment
6. The Giving of the Ten Commandments
7. Ruth, Rewarded for Conscientious Work
8. The Wicked Sons of Heli
9. The Wisdom of Solomon
10. Tobias and the Kid
11. Counsels of Tobias to his Sons
12. Martyrdom of the Seven Machabees (Youngest bribed by wealth)
13. Birth of Christ in Poverty
14. Gifts of the Magi
15. Jesus Offered in the Temple (two turtledoves)
16. Eight Beatitudes
17. Rich Young Man
18. The Unforgiving Servant
19. Rich Man and Lazarus
20. Laborers in the Vineyard
21. Zacheus
22. Mary Magdalen Anoints Jesus (Judas' hyprocrisy)
23. Tribute to Cæsar
24. Parable of the Talents
25. Barabbas, the Robber
26. Despair of Judas
27. The Last Judgment

Art Pictures for the Above Stories

The Tribute Money — *Da Vinci*
Lazarus at the Rich Man's Door — *Doré*
Christ in the Home of Peasants — *L'Hermite*
Holy Night — *Correggio*
Worship of the Magi — *Hoffmann*
Sermon on the Mount — *Hoffmann*

Christ and the Rich Young Man — *Hoffmann*

Kiss of Judas — *Geiger*

The Crucifixion — *Hoffmann*

The Israelites Passing through the Red Sea — *Raphael*

Moses Receiving the Tablets — *Raphael*

Isaac Blessing Jacob — *Doré*

The Selling of Joseph — *Schopin*

The Prodigal Son — *Molitor*

The Temptation of Christ — *Scheffer*

The Last Judgment — *Michelangelo*

Biblical Quotations

1. And if that wicked man restore the pledge, and render what he has robbed, and walk in the commandments of life, and do no unjust thing: he shall surely live and shall not die. *Ez.* xxx. 15.

2. The beginning of a good way is to do justice. *Prov.* xiv. 5.

3. Exhort servants to be obedient to their masters; not defrauding, but in all things showing good fidelity. *Tit.* ii. 9.

4. Woe to him that buildeth up his house by injustice; that will oppress his friends without cause, and will not pay him his wages. *Jer.* xx, 13.

5. Give unto him that asketh of thee and from him that would borrow of thee turn not away. *Matt.* v. 42.

6. All have turned aside into their own way, every one after his own gain, from the first even to the last. *Isa.* lvi. 2.

7. In the sweat of thy face shalt thou eat bread till thou return to the earth out of which thou wast taken. *Gen.* iii. 19.

8. Of that which remaineth give alms. *I Cor.* vi. 9.

9. The desire of money is the root of all evil. *Tim.* vi. 10.

10. You cannot serve God and Mammon.

11. We brought nothing into this world: and certainly we

can carry nothing out, but having food and wherewith to be covered, with these we are content. *I Tim.* vi. 7, 8.

12. What doth it profit a man, if he gain the whole world, and suffer the loss of his own soul? Or what exchange shall a man give for his soul? *Matt.* xvi. 26.

Quotations from Various Sources

1. If a person will not restore what he has unjustly taken, when he can restore it, he has no repentance for his sin. *St. Augustine*

2. The usurer is a murderer of the poor, for he robs them of clothing, shelter, food, drink, and means of livelihood. *St. Bernard*

3. Brave is the conqueror of the lion,
Brave is the conqueror of a world,
Braver still, who conquers self!

4. There is nothing so kingly as kindness,
There is nothing so royal as truth. *Alice Cary*

5. A good name is better than riches.

6. He, indeed, is most wealthy, who is satisfied and content.

7. It is far better to be poor and honest, than rich and dishonest.

8. Every penny that is ill gotten must be restored.

9. The dishonest penny will consume the dishonest dollar.

10. Your soul is worth more than all the money and the property of the whole world.

11. While you are stealing the money, the devil is stealing your soul.

12. Return things you have found.

13. Can you put your hand on your heart and say honestly, "I have not a single dishonest penny"?

14. Better lose than win an unfair game.

15. Do unto others as you would have them do unto you.

16. Lost time is never found again. *Franklin*
17. Honesty is the best policy. *Franklin*
18. What doth it profit to gain the world,
    Or madly to seek as our goal
    Its honors and glory, wealth and joy,
    If we lose, in the seeking, our soul?
19. The purest treasure mortal times afford
    Is — spotless reputation; that away,
    Men are but gilded loam, or painted clay. *Shakespeare*
20. Finder is very seldom keeper.

Practical Resolutions for Boys

1. I promise never to take anything from the pantry without permission.

2. I resolve never to damage any school property.

3. When I have a business, I will never use false measures.

4. If I am employed, I will use my time well.

5. If I happen to break a window when I am playing ball, I will pay for it.

6. I will avoid all gambling.

7. I resolve never to steal even a pen point.

8. I will never take money from my parents.

9. I will try to prevent other boys from stealing.

10. I will never injure others' property through meanness.

For Girls

1. I will never accept anything that I know another girl has stolen.

2. When I borrow anything, I will return it.

3. I will try to find out to whom a lost article belongs and return it.

4. I will never go to another girl's desk and look into it or handle her things without her knowledge.

5. I will give a good word now and then which might help another one not to steal.

6. I will give a good example by not stealing or damaging other's property.

7. I will not neglect to prevent theft if it is possible.

8. I resolve to tell when I see others take things which they have no right to.

9. If I cannot return something I have stolen, I will make up for it in some other way.

Bibliography

1. *Teacher's Handbook to the Catechism.* Vol. II. By Rev. A. Urban. Joseph Wagner, New York, 1903.

2. *The Commandments Explained* by Rev. Jos. Baierl. Seminary Press, Rochester, N. Y., 1920.

3. *The Catechism in Examples* by Rev. D. Chisholm. In three volumes. Vol. III, The Commandments. Burns, Oates and Washbourne, 28 Orchard St., 8–10 Paternoster Row, 1908. (These books are excellent.)

4. *Moral Series* by Rev. Rod. MacEachen. Vol. IV. *Justice and Rights.* Catholic Book Co., Wheeling, W. Va.

5. *The Holy Bible.*

6. *Sacred Heart Messenger,* April, 1929. "Mrs. Delafield's Goose"; "Tommy's Divine Chum"; and "The Hard Heart" (Jan., 1929).

7. *The Young Catholic Messenger,* "That Boy from St. Andrews."

8. *Ave Maria Stories* by Gertrude McNally all very fine, especially the "Literal Rastus Stories."

APPENDIX

The following stories are taken from *The Sacred Heart Messenger*, April 1929.

HE KISSED THE PICTURE FERVENTLY

TOMMY'S DIVINE CHUM

George M. A. Cain

Tommy closed the door before he stepped over to his bed and drew from under its pillow a round, white-framed picture with celluloid glazing. Mother had had it framed that way, so that it could not cut him, when he was so little that he must have everything he loved in bed with him.

He kissed the picture fervently. He had closed the door, because he was not sure it was not a little babyish for a nine-year-old boy to kiss that picture. Maybe it was a real sac-ra-men-tal — yes, that was the word — but maybe not the picture.

This picture represented Jesus as a Boy. You may find it in the centre of the great painting of Christ before the doctors in the Temple, by Hoffmann. You may find it, like Tommy's copy, taken away from the doctors and showing only the Holy Boy Himself.

Tommy's mother knew our Lord had come to this world to be a Boy, as well as many other things, so that all the boys in the world might find Him and love Him as their closest Friend, like themselves, One of them, the Boy of boys. That was why she had bought Tommy that picture and encouraged his devotion. He had wished for a medal like it. Mother had got it for him. It was around his neck now, on a good, strong string. He loved it better than anything else in the world.

Well he might love it. For it formed for him the picture of his God. What he prayed to oftenest and most fervently was that wondrous Boy. When he served Father Martin's early Mass, the Boy was what he saw in the uplifted Host and then received into his own breast. And he was perfectly right about that. Whatever Jesus ever was, He ever is in the Blessed Sacrament unto the consummation of the world, and at the right hand of the Father for all eternity.

TOMMY'S special fervor at this moment had a reason. A moment ago Tommy had brushed his hair to go back to school after his lunch. Very little looking in the mirror

FATHER MARTIN HAD RUN OUT FROM HIS STUDY TO HELP TOMMY TO HIS FEET

had shown the last tinge of black under his left eye. That bluish discoloration was, right now, the pride of Tommy's life. It had been a glorious fight, the first and only fight of Tommy's life. The overgrown bully of the class had risen, shrieking, from the ground at the end of that fight, to run faster than Tommy had breath left to run.

Tommy was no fighter. His mother had brought him up to know it was sinful to fight — under most circumstances. But, when Tommy had started for home last week to find big Bobby Jones actually kicking Tommy's little sister, whom he had pushed to the ground out of his way, Tommy had clutched his medal with both hands through his small blouse, and cried:

"Jesus, Jesus, help me to protect her!"

His hands had felt the strength of two boys' hands. Tommy knew he could not have stood two minutes of that fight alone; and was entirely sure the extra strength had been that of the Divine Boy to whom he had prayed. Father Martin had run out from his study to help Tommy to his feet. And he told the cheering boys around that this had been a good fight, because Tommy had fought for his sister and for what was right.

"God helped Tommy win it," Father Martin had declared. "I don't believe Tommy could have beaten Bobby alone. It was like David's fight with the giant Goliath."

Even the gentle Sisters had taken him in and washed him up and said nice things about their little David, who had done something likely to prove more effective than all their punishments of the bully.

Mother had not understood and had acted very sad about it, until Mrs. Jones had led Bobby and her husband and a big policeman around to get the terrible bully who had hurt her "darling little lambkin". One look at Bobby, a giant indeed beside Tommy, had changed mother's idea about it all; as one look at Tommy, almost four years younger and hardly half Bobby's size, had changed Mr. Jones's view, so that he had given Tommy a ten-dollar gold-piece "for doing what I ought to have done myself long ago." Of course, small Mary's bruises had been put in evidence.

TOMMY was used to Mother's approval, and Father Martin's, and, most of the time, the Sisters' who almost made a "teacher's pet" of the youngest child in his class. Something else was much more important to Tommy. He had gone to school the next morning to find himself a hero amongst the other boys of the class. He had never been a hero before. Occasionally he had heard "Sissy" applied to him. But all those boys had wanted to thrash Bobby Jones; some of the bigger ones had tried. Bobby, left over from year to year because he would not study, had finished them off easily enough. Though Tommy had answered Father Martin: "I asked Him to help me, Father," a fight is a fight, and Tommy had been the one they had seen doing ferociously and well just what they could not do.

Being such a good friend with our Lord Himself, Tommy quite naturally thought he was a good bit of a saint. It is not often that a saint can be popular with everybody of his class. Naturally Tommy liked his new position very well. And he was doing well to kiss the lovely picture in genuine thankfulness for it. Many children, and grown folk too, forget all about who helped them get their glories.

But thinking one is a saint is about the un-saintliest thing in the world. Real Saints never dream of themselves as being anything like Saints at all. Tommy needed very much to look out for himself. Spiritual pride is the most dangerous of all sins.

Tommy ran the first block of the way to school so fast, that little sister Mary had hard work to keep up. He hoped the boys would be around the front of the big building. Half way up the second block, Tommy stopped and clutched at his picture medal. Tommy had remembered something, perhaps because he could see there were no boys in front of the school. He knew he was not late.

He knew something else. A little before noon, Sister Mercedes had sent him to the basement to wash an inkstain from his hand. He had forgotten to hurry back, when the stain was gone. Instead he had done a little exploring. In a dim corner, he had come across plumber's tools. Tommy's Uncle Jack was a plumber. He always did mother's plumbing for her, and liked to tell Tommy about what he

175

was doing. Tommy knew all about plumbing, he was very sure. He knew immediately that the plumbers had gone away to get more tools or something, as plumbers almost always do. Probably they would stay out to lunch.

Down in the bottom of a little hole in the floor a valve handle stuck up straight. He wondered what that was for. He reached down to push it. It would not move for his strength. He had to show himself then that it could move. A heavy wrench with a queer end to it lay handy. He got it adjusted to the valve handle and pushed with all his might. It gave a little. Tommy called forth a little extra might and pushed harder. It went down so suddenly that Tommy fell over it. He got up and looked ruefully at his hands and knees. He went back to the washroom to clean them up.

WATER was pouring into one of the washbowls. Tommy ran toward it to shut it off, but the valve had been taken out of the faucet. He knew then, all about that cut-off he had just opened. No wonder he had not got cold water to finish washing his hand. Uncle Jack always closed the cut-off valves to put new washers into the faucets.

The plumbers must have taken the valve with them. The water was rising in that bowl and would be on the floor in a moment. Tommy rushed back to the valve in the hole. He tried again to adjust the wrench. He could not get it to work backward in such close quarters. A splash of water sounded from the washroom.

You could usually turn a valve on around and close it again — that kind of a valve. Tommy tried that, but failed. My, but that water was pouring in there!

In desperation, Tommy hit the end of the valve handle with the back of the wrench. He hit it again. A sharp

176

TOMMY HAD NEVER
SUPPOSED SO MUCH
WATER COULD POUR
OVER THE SIDE OF
ONE WASHBOWL

snap — and the handle, broken off, dropped to the bottom of the hole.

Tommy had stood up and walked twice around that hole for full realization of his helplessness. He had gone back to the washroom. The concrete floor sloped to a drain in the centre. An awful pool was growing around that drain. Tommy had never supposed so much water could pour over the side of one washbowl.

Overhead came the sound of clattering feet, boys rushing out for the noon hour. Some of them might rush down here — and catch him. Cold terror had gripped Tommy. He had taken to his heels and run up the stairs. Near the top he had almost collided with Bobby Jones.

"Hello, Tommy," Bobby had spoken meekly.

"Hello."

Tommy had tried to say it with that calm superiority he had been putting in his greetings of Bobby ever since the fight; he had barely heard his own voice.

Once upstairs, he had not gone to his classroom, empty by now anyhow. He had run right out to the street and all the way home, where he had been glad to elude his mother, as he hurried into the bathroom to wash off the greasy mud from hands and knees. Safe then from dangerous questions, he had found it easy to forget his worry, to hope that the plumbers would have got back before anything serious could result from his accident with the valve, or that the weight of water would have pressed the stoppage of the drain away——.

Oh, a lot of things could have happened to prevent any real damage. Anyway, he was safely out of it.

But now, in the middle of the block, it came back to him. Why were no boys in front of the school? The building looked grim.

Here came some one from inside! Bobby Jones, of course! If there were any trouble, Bobby would be making himself absent from it. Bobby's heavy, mean face had a pleased look on it. He came to meet Tommy without a bit of the humbleness Tommy had begun to like about him.

"Oh, Tommy, you're in for it!" he greeted now.

"In for what?" Tommy demanded sharply.

"You'll know in a minute. Father just sent me out for you. The auditorium floor is deep enough with water to swim in."

"Water!" Tommy gasped. "How did water get there?"

Tommy knew how it could get there. The auditorium, dance-floor, gymnasium, general entertainment room for all the parish affairs, was let down with a tier of seats from the sides of that floor level which went around it like a gallery, to washrooms, coatrooms, and doors to subcellars.

"Ran from the washroom where you left the water running a flood from the broken faucet, of course," Bobby accused joyously.

"Who said so?" Tommy demanded so belligerently that Bobby remembered last week and backed away from him.

"Sister said you were the last one she let go down before noon," the big boy spoke cautiously. "I didn't see anything you did, and wouldn't tell, if I had seen. I just saw you coming out in an awful hurry."

Sister! And Father Martin! Tommy clutched at his medal. He felt the cord pull about his neck.

"Better go on in," Bobby blustered, as Tommy hesitated.

The cord suddenly gave, as Tommy followed up the steps. Bobby led to the basement door inside, and down the steps.

"Somebody will have to pay for this, boys. It is going to cost about five hundred dollars," Father Martin was saying sternly. "Unless I find out now who did it, all the boys in school will stay in every afternoon until I do find out."

He was saying it from the platform of the auditorium. All the boys in school and many of the girls were sitting around the amphitheatre, looking across, not quite water enough to swim in, but too much to walk in without high rubbers.

"By the time this drains off, the floor will be ruined. We cannot hold tomorrow night's entertainment in here now. I don't know what we shall do."

He said this to one of the Sisters. They were all on the platform with him. A boy of an upper grade looked as if he had just come triumphantly through a grilling. Sister Mercedes was shaking her head mournfully.

"Come on down here, Tommy!" she called, as he appeared.

"And you may come too, Bobby Jones," Father Martin added. "A boy who is in trouble as much as you are makes himself suspicious. You're the only boy who seems even to think he knows anything about this."

"Tommy," he spoke more gently to his favorite, little altar-boy, "Sister says she sent you down to the washroom just before noon. You did not notice any water running in there, when you came down, did you?"

When he had come down! Tommy looked up.

"No, Father," he answered truthfully enough.

"Bobby says he saw you run out of the door upstairs, as if you were in a terrible hurry."

So Bobby had been careful to deny coming down at all!

"Bobby met me on the stairs," Tommy again spoke the truth. "I — I heard everybody going, and I hurried to get home."

"What stairs, Tommy?" asked the priest.

"Those over there, of course," Tommy answered. "He was about — more than half way down."

A little shock of guilt ran through Tommy. Bobby had not really reached the landing in the middle of the stair.

"O-o-oh!" Father Martin turned sharply on Bobby. "So you lied, young man; you were down there after all!"

His eyes stared like lights into Bobby's until the big boy's dropped.

"N-no — yes, Father," Bobby faltered.

Tommy's hands clutched at his blouse. Tommy wanted to pray hard — that Father would blame Bobby Jones. Bobby was not at all the first innocent to get the blame for a crime by lying out of circumstances that might seem to incriminate him. He had done just that now.

180

"Why didn't you say so before?" Father Martin demanded.

"I was scared," Bobby admitted.

"What were you scared about?"

BOBBY had to hear that question again to answer: "The water," Bobby said sullenly. "It was all over the washroom floor and running like a waterfall over the bowl. I got my feet all wet, trying to stop it; but it wouldn't turn off. There wasn't any valve in it."

"Why did you not come up and tell somebody about it?" the priest asked again.

"I always get blamed for everything around here. I'd only get myself in bad."

Bobby's voice was husky now with fear.

"I guess the rest may go to their classes now," Father Martin said slowly. "Bobby's father is a lawyer, a little better at this kind of questioning than I."

Bobby began to cry. He was too big a boy to cry. Only Sister Mercedes looked really very sorry for him. She turned to Tommy once more. He was releasing a long held breath. A terribly close call he had escaped. But, he wished he had not said Bobby was more than half way down; he reached for his beloved picture medal.

Gone!

Bobby shrieking, "I won't go. I never done it. You know my father'll half kill me rather than pay five hundred dollars!" Father Martin drew him firmly to his feet. The big baby!

But Tommy need not have exaggerated about it. And now what was Sister saying?

"Tommy, you know how serious this whole matter is. You didn't see any tools down here — a wrench or hammer or anything, did you?"

181

"No, Sister."

It was out before he thought. And the medal *was gone*. He ran his hand downward. He swept the other hand up to his neck; he thrust it inside his wide collar. Even the cord was gone.

"You didn't go into that corner back there?"

"No, Sister."

Oh, why did she keep making him tell lies like this? He did not like to tell lies.

"You're sure, Tommy?"

"Yes, Sister."

"What is it you've lost, Tommy?" Sister suddenly changed her line of questioning.

"I've lost my Jesus," he answered with quick relief from her other queries. He had always called either of the two pictures "his Jesus".

"Your what, Tommy?"

There was nothing but surprised curiosity in her tone.

"It's my medal picture of Jesus," he explained.

He was still feeling all over his blouse for it.

"Oh," she replied with a smile, "I hope you haven't lost Jesus Himself."

He started to smile back at her. The smile died on his face. Why did Sister still look at him that way? What did she mean by her questions? Lost Jesus Himself? But had he? He had lied and lied again about his own guilt. He was letting another boy go to only Heaven knew what punishment for his fault. He had even tried to make Bobby appear guilty. That, was a bad sin of injustice. Tommy remembered the way Bobby's father had looked at his son after the fight. Bobby might well cry now.

WHY DID SISTER STILL LOOK AT HIM THAT WAY?

"Well, come on, Tommy," Sister was saying. "Your medal is not on the platform. We all lose our medals sometimes."

His medal? Was that all he had lost? He could go on and live without the medal, at least so long as he had the larger picture by his bed. But — the Boy Himself! — No, Jesus would never have done this even to bad Bobby. Jesus could not stay friends with Tommy so different from Himself.

"Come, Tommy!"

Sister's voice was commanding now. Father had got Bobby marched up to the higher level. And Bobby's father would half kill the lad.

Well, Tommy would have to get Father to hear his Confession tomorrow morning. No, he could not confess this to Father Martin. He would have to wait until Saturday and go to the assistant. Only Father Martin loved the little altar-boy well enough to respond to his call any morning after Tommy had "hurt Jesus's feelings", as he had once worded his plea to be heard before Mass.

Five whole days to Sunday! Could he endure them without his precious Friend? Could Confession alone bring back that Friend? Bobby would have taken his punishment by then. Tommy could never undo that. His child mind could not quite see how Jesus would ever fix him up fit for their old comradeship again.

JESUS gone! Was this what happened when one committed a sin of injustice? The thing was done, and could not be undone, and, even if Jesus did come back, you would always have to remember and He would always know that somewhere was another of His children you had hurt. And Jesus must always feel a little for the hurt child, a little as the hurt one felt toward him. This hurt

184

to Jesus must last and last, until the injury was undone. Tommy could see no other way about it. It would not take Father Martin long to summon a taxi and get Bobby down to Mr. Jones's office, and then——

"Poor Bobby!" Sister seemed to speak his very thoughts.

Inwardly she knew full well that Father would never take the boy to his father yet. Father Martin was acquainted enough with Bobby's father to trust his own quizzing rather than the lawyer's anger.

But Tommy could not know that. Father Martin drew the struggling Bobby through the door to his own basement. It closed. But Bobby's wails still rang in Tommy's ears. Poor Bobby!

MUCH rather, poor Tommy! At the worst, Bobby could get no more than bodily bruises from an undeserved beating. Tommy was spoiling his Friendship with God! Tommy might be quite sure he could be forgiven somehow; he was equally sure this thing must forever remain a hurt to his Divine Chum's feelings. Their Friendship could never again be quite the same.

And it had been so lovely. When he had first got that picture, his lively little imagination had made a regular playmate of this Divine Boy. He had asked Jesus to help him climb trees, and had got up them. He had never been afraid of anything with that Almighty young Friend of his. Even now at his present mature age, he never stood up with a bat in his hand before a pitcher, without touching that precious medal-picture at his breast. He had been sure that was why he made so many hits in games where errors never are counted, but almost any hit is a home run before the scrambling youngsters manage to do anything about it.

185

FIVE days without that Friend at all! The rest of all those days with that Friend still feeling badly about this! Suppose he should die before Saturday!

"Father! Father!"

Tommy had stopped at the door. He could not stand it.

"Come, Tommy," Sister bade again. "You must not bother Father now."

"Oh, but, Sister — Sister — I — I — did it."

No matter though she and the school would know that he had been a cheap, cowardly liar, instead of the smug little saint. He must have back his Friend. He knocked hard. The door opened.

"Bobby deserved that scare for trying to tattle on you," Father Martin explained later. "I don't like tattling. Now, what am I to do to you?"

"Beat me, Father—the way Bobby's father would beat him. Oh, Father, I deserve it. I tried to make you think Bobby had done it---"

"Yes, that was your real sin, Tommy. I am very sorry about the floor. I can hardly make your poor mother pay for the serious damage. I certainly hope you will never tamper with things again this way. But I shan't beat you. It's quite out of my line."

Of course Bobby had been sent upstairs, quite vindicated.

"As a reparation to your Friend take that lovely picture of yours and tell your dear Boy Friend how sorry you really are——"

His look at the floor checked him. There at Tommy's feet lay the medal, as it had finally fallen clear through his clothes.

"I THOUGHT I HAD LOST HIM," TOMMY CRIED WITH ASTONISHMENT

"I thought I had lost Him," Tommy cried with astonishment.

"I am not surprised that you thought so, when you let me drag Bobby this far, Tommy," Father Martin replied soberly. "I knew by your face all the while that you had done it. The worst is that He knew too. I only wanted to reprimand Bobby for lying."

But Tommy was passionately kissing the picture with no thought of embarrassment. Father Martin was not sure that Tommy had heard the last remark at all.

MRS. DELAFIELD'S
DISDAINFUL GLANCE
SWEPT HIM FROM
HEAD TO FOOT

MRS. DELAFIELD'S GOOSE

Vara Macbeth Jones

O H, MRS. DELAFIELD, the goose's gone!"
Hattie Squires, the middle-aged servant in the household, burst through the back door with the dire news, perturbation written all over her good-natured face. Laura Delafield, standing by the table in the big, sunny kitchen, had just thrust the last of thirty-five pink candles in the roseholders on a three-layer, frosted cake, and was gazing on her

creation with admiring countenance. But at the words her complacency fled, her pretty face wrinkling anxiously.

"Gone!" she echoed aghast. "Why, I don't see how it could get away. You shut it in the garage, didn't you?"

"Yes'm, and closed the door tight, far as I know. But now it's swingin' a little open, and that goose ain't in sight. I've gone all over the place, too." She turned toward the back door again, but rather uncertainly. "I guess I might as well go look some more, though it don't seem much use."

"Well, we've just got to find it," her mistress insisted, as she slipped her frilled white apron from her dainty lavender house-dress and followed in the older woman's wake. "It wouldn't be Mr. Delafield's birthday dinner without his favorite roast goose, and it's certainly too late for me to get into market and out again, especially with the car being repaired, and the afternoon trains so few and far between. Come on! We'll scour the grounds."

THE Delafield home, a charming, rambling cottage, stood in a big sweep of lawn and orchard in a little community of equally attractive suburban homes, twelve miles or more from the city where Christopher Delafield practised law. The garage was some distance from the house, screened by a row of poplars. With hurrying footsteps the two women approached it. But Hattie's words were only too true. The interior was empty. The big goose the master had sent out from market for his birthday feast had disappeared.

"I can't understand it!" Mrs. Delafield exclaimed. "Have you seen anybody about the grounds?"

"No'm," Hattie said thoughtfully. "Far as I know there ain't been a soul stopped by here today, 'ceptin' the market fellow and his truck. And a few minutes after he put the crate on the back porch I went out and got it and carried it down here."

"Well, then, you must have left the door unlatched, and the goose has wandered off," Mrs. Delafield insisted accusingly.

"I was sure I shut it tight," Hattie defended worriedly. "I saw right away that fowl was the wild kind that needed close pennin' up. I know, when I was gettin' it out of the crate, it gave a flyin' leap and made a wild dash for the orchard, and if it hadn't been for one of the Watson youngsters bein' in the back field and shooin' it through the fence, goodness knows if I'd ever caught up with it."

AT the words her mistress suddenly straightened, her gaze turning on a tiny, whitewashed house, little more than a shack, in a field beyond the orchard boundary. Instantly her black eyes narrowed suspiciously.

"Well, now I begin to see daylight," she exclaimed knowingly. "So one of that Watson crew was around, when you put the goose away. Which one was it?"

"Young Ned, huntin' firewood." Then Hattie shook a vehement head in response to her mistress's unspoken accusation. "But, 'deed, Mrs. Delafield, I don't believe them kids would take a blade of grass. Why, I ain't even seen them on this side of the road since you blamed them for robbin' your orchard."

Mrs. Delafield smiled scornfully.

"Oh, Hattie, you're just like Mr. Delafield, where those Watsons are concerned. So gullible you make me laugh. But I'm not such an easy mark. You go back to the house and put a big pot of water on to heat, and see if I don't bring that goose back, or some clue to its mysterious disappearance."

Without further ado she went across the orchard, letting herself out the back gate. Old Hattie gazed after the determined figure.

"I ain't never seen a human being so quick to suspicion people as Mrs. Delafield," she told herself regretfully. "And it ain't right, nohow. She can talk all she likes about the master bein' easy, but I just call it bein' Christianlike, if you was to ask me."

In the meantime, Mrs. Delafield was continuing on her way across the field to the tiny house, her eyes flashing, her lips grim. The Watson family did not stand

OLD HATTIE GAZED AFTER THE DETERMINED FIGURE

very high in her favor. They had been living in the shack when the community was first developed, and the real estate company had allowed them to remain on as tenants, as long as that particular plot of ground was not sold. There was a large family of them, eight in all, with the children ranging in steps from Veenie, a thin, undernourished child of thirteen, down to Buddy, the baby of less than a year. The father, Joe Watson, was a simple, rather pathetic, type, a most willing worker, but wholly unskilled, and compelled to take such odd jobs as he could find. His wife, a brisk, energetic, little soul, supplemented the family income by laundry and day's work.

But even such a meagre livelihood as their united efforts gave them was to be denied them. Some six months back, Joe, who had been serving as a substitute night-watchman at a nearby canning factory, had been arrested as a suspect in connection with the disappearance of a crate of food from the premises, was convicted despite his protests of innocence, and sentenced to three years in the workhouse.

It was at this time that Christopher Delafield's interest in the family was aroused. Believing in Joe's innocence, he fought his case in court for him, lost it — but, still undaunted — was still putting forth an effort to bring about his client's vindication and release. All of which was in keeping with what his wife considered his too trusting nature, and met with her usual chiding and scoffing.

"You're entirely too Quixotic, my dear," she had insisted. "I haven't the slightest doubt, nor has any one else, but that Joe Watson stole that crate of corn. But just because he cried a little, and said he didn't do it, you're ready to champion him. I often marvel how you, after your years of experience in criminal court, can still be so gullible."

And in turn her husband repeated what he so often said, when a question of judgment was at stake:

"It's because of that very experience, my dear, that I dare not foster a suspicious nature, or judge rashly. Jumping at conclusions, refusing to give the benefit of the doubt, has brought about more unhappiness and suffering than anything else in the world. I've always suspected that that was the particular trait the poet had in mind when he wrote those lines about "Man's inhumanity to man'."

And now, with the disappearance of her goose under such suspicious circumstances, Mrs. Delafield's mind turned on her husband's words, and despite her loss, she could not help but feel a sense of righteous justification.

"Well, Christopher can let the Watsons pull the wool over his eyes if he likes, but that crew will find that I'm not so soft," she told herself emphatically, as she mounted the front steps of the shack, and knocked at the front door. There was a scurrying of footsteps down the hallway, and then Ned himself, a sandy-headed, blue-eyed, little lad of eleven, opened it.

"Where's your mother?" Mrs. Delafield asked sharply.

"She's house-cleaning for some lady in town, and won't be home till real late," the boy informed her.

"I wanted to find out if any of you had seen our big, white goose, the one you helped Hattie catch this morning," Mrs. Delafield went on pointedly, fixing her listener with a severe glance.

SHE immediately noted the latter's reaction to her question. His face suddenly flushed, his glance wavered.

"No ma'am, we — we ain't seen nothin' of — of your goose," he answered hesitatingly.

Mrs. Delafield's disdainful glance swept him from head to foot.

"You're sure of that?" she countered. Then, without waiting for a reply: "Where's Veenie? I think I prefer to talk to her about this."

At which the lad became even more perturbed.

"Veenie, she's — she's awful busy right now, Mrs. Delafield."

His uneasy glance had turned toward the back of the house; but he resolutely barred his caller's way, neither

193

making a move to admit her, or call his sister; which was entirely too much for the now thoroughly aroused woman.

"Well, I'm going to see her," she insisted, and brushing past the boy she hurried down the bare passageway and threw open the kitchen door.

Then she stood stock still. For in the squalid, little room, cluttered with children and rickety furniture, Veenie Watson stood at a table, plucking white feathers from a big, fat goose. Mrs. Delafield could not believe her eyes.

"Veenie!" she demanded, "where did you get that bird?"

The girl's thin, freckled, little face went pale under the unexpected visitor's vehemence.

"Why, somebody — somebody sent it to us," she stammered.

"Sent it to you!" Mrs. Delafield retorted. "Who was it?"

"I don't know," Veenie admitted, as she turned from her task to pick up the now crying baby, and wave the other three little ones back to their play in a corner. "Our Ned found it this morning in a crate on the front steps. And Mamma's name was on it."

"Where's the crate?" Mrs. Delafield demanded quickly.

Ned, who had followed her into the kitchen, took up the question:

"We burned it up to help heat the oven, so we can roast the goose for supper," he said defiantly.

"Glib little liar," Mrs. Delafield said to herself indignantly. Then, aloud:

"OUR NED FOUND IT THIS MORNING IN A CRATE ON THE FRONT STEPS"

194

"Well, I don't believe a word of it! We had a goose just like this one delivered this morning, and now it has disappeared."

THEN she broke off, her gaze dilated. She had just caught sight of a little tag affixed to the fowl's leg. She reached out, turning it over. "Brill Poultry Market", it read. Brill! — Her own marketman!

"No, I certainly don't believe a word of it," she repeated hotly. "Look, here's the tag, from the very firm that sent out my goose. How do you account for that? Not to mention the fact that Ned Watson was the only person about, when Hattie was taking our fowl out of the crate to put it in the garage!"

Veenie Watson stared with frightened gaze at the tag the angry visitor thrust in front of her.

"I — I don't know, Mrs. Delafield," she gulped.

"You don't know!" returned Mrs. Delafield indignantly. "And I don't suppose you know, either, how wrong it is for children to steal and lie——"

Veenie's shoulders began to shake at that.

"Oh, Mrs. Delafield, if you think the goose belongs to you, you can take it," she sobbed.

And then an unexpected thing happened. Ned suddenly placed himself between his sister and their visitor.

"We ain't thieves, and we ain't liars!" he said with flashing eyes. "And you can't come over here and say so — or help yourself to our goose, either."

With that he pounced upon the bird, whirled about, and went sprinting down the hall. With a surprised exclamation Mrs. Delafied started after him, Veenie, with the fat baby still in her arms, bringing up the rear. By the time they reached the front door, Ned's darting form could be glimpsed disappearing toward a wood some distance off. Laura Delafield's first impulse was to follow that flying figure. But her better sense came to her rescue. It would not only be a ridiculous thing to do, but an equally futile effort. Instead, she turned to Veenie Watson with tightening lips.

LAURA DELAFIELD'S FIRST IMPULSE WAS TO FOLLOW THAT FLYING FIGURE

"Well, if your brother thinks he can carry off things in that high handed way, he's badly mistaken," she declared in a tense voice. "All I have to do is go over home and call up the police. There's a motorcycle corp down the boulevard you know."

Veenie looked stricken at the threat.

"Oh, please, Mrs. Delafield, you wouldn't do that! Ned wouldn't have run off with the goose, only he hates so bad to give it up! Y'see, my papa, he's comin' home tonight; they ain't a'goin' to keep him in that old jail any more, and we was awful anxious to have a nice supper for him. But all we've got in the house is potatoes, and Mama can't even take what she's gettin' for house-cleanin' 'cause it's owed for rent. And just when we was wonderin' what we'd do, Ned found the goose, and we thought maybe God had sent it, 'cause we prayed for Him to please send us somethin'

196

nice, but now — now, we can't have nothin' but — potato soup —" and Veenie's words trailed off in hopeless sobbing.

Mrs. Delafield might have relented at that; but the girl's unfortunate reference to her father now only added to the other's sense of grievance. So her husband had succeeded in securing Joe Watson's pardon — and his family was going to celebrate by stealing their benefactor's birthday goose. She put her thoughts into words:

"Well, Veenie," she said severely, "no matter what your excuse is, stealing is stealing. And while you may have had no actual share in taking my goose, you must have known that Ned didn't come by it honestly. And that fowl was for Mr. Delafield's birthday dinner tonight, too. And if it wasn't for him, your papa wouldn't be coming home tonight. Do you wonder that I'm angry? Ned Watson deserves to have the police after him for such lack of gratitude!"

The child dashed one red, bony, little hand across her eyes.

"It'll just about kill my mama and papa, if they come home and find Neddie's been — locked up," she whispered tremulously.

Mrs. Delafield stood for the moment lost in thought.

"I'll tell you," she finally conceded. "If your brother brings back my goose, right away, I won't have him arrested this time. But I still think he deserves to go to the Juvenile Court for what he has done!"

WITH that she turned and started across the field homeward. Hattie, in the kitchen, lowering the fire under a bubbling pot of water, looked up with questioning gaze, as her mistress stalked into the kitchen.

"No, I haven't got it," the latter announced brusquely; "but it's just as I suspected. Those young thieves got our goose."

197

And she related her experience. Hattie shook a puzzled head.

"It does look black against them," she admitted. "Still, I just can't imagine them doin' a thing like that——"

"Well, we won't stand here arguing now on that point," the other woman retorted. "There's been too much time wasted already, and dinner but a few hours off. I'm going right ahead with my preparations, and if that Ned Watson doesn't let me have the fowl — and within the next half hour — I'll do just what I said: have the police round him up."

But it was in little less than half the allotted time that footsteps crossed the back porch, and Ned Watson, goose in hand, confronted Mrs. Delafield across the doorstep.

"Here — you can have it," he said briefly, holding out the bird.

But his gaze was unwavering, his little jaw grim. Certainly his attitude was not all that Mrs. Delafield expected.

"Well, you are a bold one!" she scolded indignantly. "Aren't you even going to say you're sorry, or ashamed?"

The ragged child shook his sandy head.

"No, ma'am, I ain't going to say any such thing. I ain't got nothin' to be ashamed of. I told you the truth all along, even if you don't believe me. And if it wasn't for what Veenie told me when I came back to the house, that the goose you had was for Mr. Delafield's birthday, I wouldn't be here now. But, if it was for him, then he's welcome to ours — 'cause he's — he's a prince!"

Then the defiant young voice broke suddenly at the mention of Christopher Delafield's name, and with a furtive dab at his suddenly watering eyes, he turned and fled. Hattie looked after the little figure pityingly.

"I tell you, Mrs. Delafield, I still don't b'lieve——" she began again.

But her mistress waved her words aside.

"I don't care what you believe," she exclaimed tartly. "All I care about now is getting at that dinner. Mr. Delafield expects to come out on the six o'clock express, maybe earlier, if he can make it. Though, goodness knows, with all we have yet to prepare, I'm tempted to hope that for once he will be a little late."

AND Laura Delafield's wish was to be granted. For some hours later, as she hovered over the dining-room table, which looked charming in its festal array of gleaming china, cut flowers, and cunning, little birthday favors, the telephone rang, and her husband's voice greeted her on the wire.

"Honey," he said contritely, "I'm afraid I'm going to be late tonight. I've had a big day, with things cropping up at the last minute that just had to be attended to."

At this juncture his wife could not resist shooting her barbed shaft.

"I suppose it all had something to do with that Joe Watson's pardon. I heard that he was expected home tonight. It's a wonder you wouldn't have told me about it."

There was a slight pause. Then:

"Well, if I didn't mention it, Laura, it was only because I knew you weren't very much in sympathy with my efforts. But, at any rate, thank Heaven, the man has been exonerated at last, and is on his way home by now."

Laura Delafield laughed a trifle cuttingly. This was her opportunity to say, "I told you so!"

"Well, my dear, maybe you will find there is some reason for my seeming lack of — er — sympathy. I don't think any of that Watson crew is worth your time. Why, while you have been laboring so ardently in behalf of the father, his children have been just as busy out here, stealing your birthday goose to celebrate the prodigal's return."

And again Mrs. Delafield recounted the incident of the lost fowl; or rather, started to relate it. For suddenly her husband's voice cut in on her narrative:

"But listen, Laura, there is a mistake all round. I'll have to 'fess up to something else. This morning, when I told Brill to send out our bird, I ordered one for the Watsons, too. You see, I hated to think of that poor devil walking in on them tonight, and maybe not a bite in the house to eat——"

"Christopher! But I don't understand," Mrs. Delafield stammered. "You say you sent them one — but, even so — what happened to ours?"

"Why, he probably got away," surmised her husband.

The proof of his surmise was soon forthcoming. Scarcely had Mrs. Delafield turned away from the telephone, when she heard old Hattie's surprised ejaculations from the back yard, and the next moment Hattie came rushing into her presence, a squawking goose under her arm.

"Mrs. Delafield, what do you think? I've found that ornery bird — under the back porch hidin'. It must'a been I didn't get that garage shut tight after all." Her countenance was crestfallen. "And just look what a peck of trouble it's got everybody in."

But her mistress did not seem inclined to dwell on any of Hattie's culpability.

"Oh, well, Hattie, we all make mistakes. I know I certainly made a greater one than yours this day. You see, Mr. Delafield sent a goose to the Watsons, when he sent ours. If that doesn't put me in a nice position."

She stood for a moment staring into space. Then she threw back her shoulders.

"BLESSED ARE THE POOR!"

Giles Black, O.P.

IT WAS the year of grace 1400 and six o'clock on a summer's evening. The sun blazed down on the village green where stood the Cross. Indeed there was no shade at all except alongside the church. On the steps of the Cross sat an aged friar, brown-frocked, barefooted, bearded. When the bell rang for Ave Maria, he knelt and prayed. Then he sat down again, and gathering some children round him began to teach them the simple, homely truths of God and His dear love.

It was not long before the menfolk of the village, but just returned from the fields, began to gather. Mine host of the inn stood at his door with welcome shining from his jolly, red face. But before any of the men had time to respond to his invitation, the friar's strong voice rang out from beneath the Cross.

WHEN THE BELL BANG FOR "AVE MARIA"
HE KNELT AND PRAYED

"Stay a few short moments, my brothers, and hear good words about our dear God."

The men wondered, for the friar looked old and feeble, and yet his voice was strong and young. They gathered near him; others soon came and a crowd was formed. Now that he had his audience near him, the friar spoke more softly and gently.

"*Beati pauperes spiritu, quoniam ipsorum est regnum coelorum.*" "Blessed are the poor in spirit: for theirs is the Kingdom of Heaven."

He told them how our Blessed Lord, to avoid the crowds, went up into a mountain and there preached — how He pronounced eight Beatitudes and promised a reward to each and all who should attain to any of them; each Beatitude had its own reward. He went on:

"Tonight I want to speak to you about the first, 'Blessed are the poor in spirit: for theirs is the Kingdom of Heaven'. Now, my children, to be poor in spirit means that you do not love or cling to earthly things, worldly things, things of time. The rich man, who lives in his castle and has lands and horses and cattle and many possessions, can be — must be — poor in spirit, if he is to be truly rich and possess the Kingdom of Heaven. The poor man in his cottage, with his few possessions and many trials, must be poor in spirit also, nor cling to the few things that he has, if he is to be truly rich and possess the Kingdom of Heaven."

Suddenly the friar rose to his feet and flung his arms wide:

"Dear children of Christ our Lord," he cried, "this good news I bring to you, that God has favored you and me in giving us poverty in this world, because it is easier, far easier, for us who are poor, to become poor in spirit and thus to possess the Kingdom of Heaven.

"It is hard for the rich man, easy for the poor man; for we who are poor have no earthly riches to wean us from Christ. Herein I say God has favored us. Praised be Jesus Christ!"

He stood thus a moment or two with his arms wide extended, and there was silence, except for the cry of a child some way off and the barking of a dog. Then his arms fell to his sides.

"Will any good man give me a night's lodging for God's love?" he asked.

"I will," said Diccon.

* * *

THE friar went into the church to pray, while Diccon made for home to prepare his wife for their guest.

"Margery," said he, "there is a friar in the village and he preached good things, and made me happy, and I asked him to come home for the night."

"Oh, Diccon dear, wherever shall we put him and what shall we give him to eat?"

"Put him?" said Diccon. "He isn't a prelate; he is just a poor man like us. He can sleep among the clean straw in the shed and eat bread and cheese and drink some ale. He will be quite contented. Don't you fret, dear."

Margery began to get supper ready, talking all the time.

"I thought there was some preacher at the Cross," she said. "I could hear his voice once or twice."

"Oh, that would be the time he stood up and said God was so good to us poor folk."

"What did he mean?"

"I can't just say what he meant," said Diccon, scratching

his head; "but he said how it was easier for us poor folk to be poor and — and — but he'll tell you himself when he comes."

"It doesn't sound sense, Diccon, but you just go and fetch the poor man. He'll be right welcome and maybe he'll tell us what he meant."

* * *

WHEN Diccon left the village green, the friar, hand-in-hand with a little maid of some four years, went into the church.

"Turn round here," said the child.

"Round here" was the shrine of our Blessed Lady. The statue was of painted wood, dressed in silken cope and gilded crown.

The two, still hand-in-hand, knelt down, and the old man began to speak of our Mother's love, but soon his eyes gazed out into the far distance and his face became radiant and smiling. He stopped speaking. The child looked up at him and decided that he was not going to talk any more; so she repeated what she had just heard to a rag doll of doubtful beauty, which she was carrying in her arms.

Thus Diccon found them — the friar, lips parted and eyes smiling, the child a little frightened and restless now.

"Father!" said Diccon.

But there was no answer.

"Father!"

Louder this time and accompanied with a shake of the shoulders.

"Ah!" said the friar. "Where — oh, yes, I know. You have come for me. Well, little one, we will all go together. Where does she live?"

"It is a neighbor's child. We will take her home on our way."

AFTER they had supped, Diccon said:

"Father, will you tell Margery here what you said on the green. You said how God had given us poor folk something the rich had not."

The friar smiled.

"Yes, willingly," he replied. He turned to Margery and went on: "I was saying that God wants to make us all rich one day in Heaven. But to become rich we must be poor in this life. Now to be poor in this life means not to love and cling to earthly possessions. See then how good God is to us poor folk. It is much easier not to love earthly goods, if we are without them. I am not speaking so much of those who are sunk in gross sins against the law of God, as of those, who, because they possess many things — lands, horses, earthly goods — find it very hard not to root their hearts in these things, and very difficult to wish for anything better, and very, very bitter to have to die and leave them.

"Listen, while I tell you a story," the old man continued.

"Once upon a time there was a very rich noble. He had lands and goods and many possessions. One day he went out hunting and fell from his horse. He was brought home dying.

"His son, a lad of twenty, sent for the priest, but for a very long time the dying man refused to make his Confession and prepare for his going forth to God. Why? He was not a bad man, but life had been very pleasant. He had never wanted for anything. He had had few troubles and but little sickness. He had not even been touched by the sorrows of others. He gave alms to the poor and fed them, but always by means of his servants.

"Well, the priest stayed by him and spoke of the vanity of earthly things, of the riches that await us in Heaven and of the need of bowing to God's holy will and making a good death, if he were ever to gain those riches.

"It was of no avail. The rich man turned his face away.

"But all this time the young lad, his son, was listening and thinking.

He had never seen death before, never before had he thought deeply of things and weighed them.

"He said to himself: I am heir to all those great possessions. I am also heir to the Kingdom of Heaven. I must covet Heavenly riches, but on earthly riches I may not set my heart. How hard this will be for me! What shall I do?'

"Then our Blessed Lord looked on him and loving him much put this thought in his heart — to leave these earthly things of his own free will, now, before he learned to love them, and so make more sure of his Heavenly heirdom.

"Thus, as the dying man still lay, refusing all comfort and priestly help, the boy lifted his eyes to a picture of our Lord, and so gave himself that, if it should be God's will, he would be poor and a friar. At that moment his father turned and asked to make his Confession and receive the Sacraments. A few hours after he died in peace."

The friar paused and then again went on:

"I am telling you this not because I want you to think that the rich and the noble cannot enter the Kingdom of Heaven, but that you who are poor may see that your poverty is a help to you from God. At least it should be so."

"And what happened to the boy, Father?" they both asked.

"Oh, he became a poor friar and I hope a useful one. God knows, who knows all."

HIS LIPS PARTED AND A LOOK OF WONDER CAME OVER HIM

"Did you ever meet him?"

"Oh, yes. I knew him well; indeed, I still do."

"Did he never regret all he had given up?"

This was from Margery.

"No, my child, never."

The friar smiled, and his gaze seemed to be fixing on something invisible, but infinitely lovely. His lips parted and a look of wonder came over him. But suddenly he stood up.

"I must go and rest," he said.

Diccon led him out to the back, to a little shed, where there was an abundance of clean, fresh straw, and there he made him warm and comfortable for the night.

"I will say Mass very early in the morning, kind friend," said the friar, "and go on my way."

* * *

DICCON went with the Father next morning to serve his Mass, and it was at the moment of the showing of the Host that God spoke. The priest adored, then raised the Host that all might see. He held it some moments aloft, as if for him time was standing still.

Diccon looked up to say his prayer, "My Lord and my God." But somehow he never said it, for, at the back of his simple, childlike mind, there flashed before him that he who held there in his hands, the Giver of all riches, was one who had given up great possessions that he might enter the Kingdom of Heaven, and in so doing had brought peace of soul to a dying man. When Mass was over, Diccon said:

"I know Father now, who the young man was you told us about."

"Ah, well," said the friar, "don't tell any one."

"Not Margery, Father?"

"No one else."

Diccon fairly ran home, laughing to himself. One or two of the men saw him and said:

"Diccon be surely going mad."

"Margery!" he cried. "It was himself."

"Who was himself?"

Then Diccon told her.

They had always been contented and happy, those two, but from now onwards I think they better knew why. The poor in spirit shall inherit the Kingdom of Heaven.

www.ingramcontent.com/pod-product-compliance
Lightning Source LLC
LaVergne TN
LVHW011347080426
835511LV00005B/179